Anonymous

General Orders Affecting the Volunteer Force

Adjutant General's Office, 1862

Anonymous

General Orders Affecting the Volunteer Force
Adjutant General's Office, 1862

ISBN/EAN: 9783337779191

Printed in Europe, USA, Canada, Australia, Japan

Cover: Foto ©Suzi / pixelio.de

More available books at **www.hansebooks.com**

GENERAL ORDERS

AFFECTING

THE VOLUNTEER FORCE.

ADJUTANT GENERAL'S OFFICE.

1862.

————•————

WASHINGTON:
GOVERNMENT PRINTING OFFICE.
1863.

INDEX OF SUBJECTS.

NOTE. The *figures* refer to the *number* of the orders; the *dates*, to *circulars* and *orders* not numbered.

2

3

GENERAL ORDERS, } HEADQUARTERS OF THE ARMY,
ADJUTANT GENERAL'S OFFICE,
No. 1. *Washington, January 6, 1862.*

I..Transportation by Express Agency being liable to abuse, and very expensive, is prohibited by the Secretary of War, on public account, except in cases of great emergency.

II..The power given in *" General Orders,"* Nos. 58 and 61, of 1861, to Volunteer Officers to muster volunteers into service, is hereby revoked. They may, however, receive volunteer recruits into service on enlistments.

BY COMMAND OF MAJOR GENERAL McCLELLAN :

L. THOMAS,
Adjutant General.

GENERAL ORDERS, } HEADQUARTERS OF THE ARMY,
ADJUTANT GENERAL'S OFFICE,
No. 3. *Washington, January 11, 1862.*

¤   ¤   ¤   ¤   ¤   ¤   ¤   ¤

II..Officers detailed for the Volunteer Recruiting Service, under *" General Orders,"* No. 105, of 1861, are to recruit for their own regiments, respectively, and not for the General Volunteer Service. They will, however, be under the direction of the General Superintendent.

The full number of officers indicated for Recruiting Service need not be detailed if a less number will suffice to fill up the several regiments. The selections will be made by the Colonels, and the order for detail given by Commanders of Departments or *Corps d Armeé.*

BY COMMAND OF MAJOR GENERAL McCLELLAN :

L. THOMAS,
Adjutant General.

GENERAL ORDERS, } HEADQUARTERS OF THE ARMY,
ADJUTANT GENERAL'S OFFICE,
No. 4. *Washington January 18, 1862.*

I..Under instructions from the Secretary of War, dated January 7, 1862, guidons and camp colors for the Army will be made like the United States flag, with stars and stripes.

¤   ¤   ¤   ¤   ¤   ¤   ¤   ¤

III..Commutation in lieu of rations in kind will not be paid to recruiting parties while at their stations. This is not intended to interfere with a strict construction of the regulations affecting enlisted men while travelling.

     o   o   o   o   o   o   o

BY COMMAND OF MAJOR GENERAL McCLELLAN:

L. THOMAS,

Adjutant General.

GENERAL ORDERS,	HEADQUARTERS OF THE ARMY,
No. 7.	ADJUTANT GENERAL'S OFFICE, *Washington, January 29, 1862.*

By direction of the Secretary of War, private letters received by officers of the Army for transmittal through the lines of the United States troops to persons living in the enemy's country, will not hereafter be forwarded, but will be sent to the Dead Letter Office, in the city of Washington. Exception to this rule is made in favor of letters addressed to officers and men detained as prisoners by the insurgents.

BY COMMAND OF MAJOR GENERAL McCLELLAN:

L. THOMAS,

Adjutant General.

GENERAL ORDERS,	HEADQUARTERS OF THE ARMY,
No. 9.	ADJUTANT GENERAL'S OFFICE, *Washington February 1, 1862.*

     o   o   o   o   o   o   o

II..The Secretary of War directs that officers and soldiers of the United States, who are or may be prisoners of war, shall, during their imprisonment, be considered entitled to and receive the same pay as if they were doing active duty.

BY COMMAND OF MAJOR GENERAL McCLELLAN:

L. THOMAS,

Adjutant General.

GENERAL ORDERS, } HEADQUARTERS OF THE ARMY,
ADJUTANT GENERAL'S OFFICE,
No. 10. } *Washington, February 4, 1862.*

The following act of Congress is published for the information of all concerned:

AN ACT to authorize the President of the United States in certain cases to take possession of railroad and telegraph lines, and for other purposes.

*Be it enacted by the Senate and House of Representatives of the United States
of America in Congress assembled,* That the President of the United States,
when in his judgment the public safety may require it, be, and he is
hereby, authorized to take possession of any or all the telegraph lines
in the United States, their offices and appurtenances; to take possession
of any or all the railroad lines in the United States, their rolling stock,
their offices, shops, buildings, and all their appendages and appurtenances ; to prescribe rules and regulations for the holding, using, and
maintaining of the aforesaid telegraph and railroad lines, and to extend, repair, and complete the same, in the manner most conducive to
the safety and interest of the Government; to place under military
control all the officers, agents, and employés belonging to the telegraph
and railroad lines thus taken possession of by the President, so that
they shall be considered as a post road and a part of the military
establishment of the United States, subject to all the restrictions imposed by the Rules and Articles of War.

SEC. 2. *And be it further enacted,* That any attempt by any party or
parties whomsoever, in any State or District in which the laws of the
United States are opposed, or the execution thereof obstructed by insurgents and rebels against the United States, too powerful to be sup-
pressed by the ordinary course of judicial proceedings, to resist or
interfere with the unrestrained use by Government of the property
described in the preceding section, or any attempt to injure or destroy
the property aforesaid, shall be punished as a military offence, by
death, or such other penalty as a Court Martial may impose.

SEC. 3. *And be it further enacted,* That three commissioners shall be
appointed by the President of the United States, by and with the
advice and consent of the Senate, to assess and determine the damages

suffered, or the compensation to which any railroad or telegraph company may be entitled by reason of the railroad or telegraph line being seized and used under the authority conferred by this act, and their award shall be submitted to Congress for their action.

SEC. 4. *And be it further enacted,* That the transportation of troops, munitions of war, equipments, military property and stores, throughout the United States, shall be under the immediate control and supervision of the Secretary of War and such agents as he may appoint; and all rules, regulations, articles, usages, and laws in conflict with this provision are hereby annulled.

SEC. 5 *And be it further enacted,* That the compensation of each of the commissioners aforesaid shall be eight dollars per day while in actual service; and that the provisions of this act, so far as it relates to the operating and using said railroads and telegraphs, shall not be in force any longer than is necessary for the suppression of this rebellion.

Approved January 31, 1862.

BY COMMAND OF MAJOR GENERAL McCLELLAN:

L. THOMAS,

Adjutant General.

GENERAL ORDERS, }   HEADQUARTERS OF THE ARMY.

                          ADJUTANT GENERAL'S OFFICE,

No. 12. }   *Washington, February 6, 1862.*

The following orders are from the War Department:

The Department has been so frequently embarrassed by the action of General Officers of the Volunteer service, in appointing or giving acting appointments to persons to serve upon their staff, that it becomes necessary to issue a general notice to all whom it may concern, that no such appointments can be, or will be, recognized by the Government.

The President, alone, by and with the advice and consent of the Senate, has power to make any appointment in the Army. To no General has he delegated any portion of this power. From the War Department, through the Adjutant General of the Army, all notices of appointment issue, and none other are valid.

The Assistant Adjutant General of every Division; the Assistant Adjutant General, Assistant Quartermaster, Commissary of Subsistence, Surgeon, and Paymaster of each Brigade of volunteers will be regularly assigned to it from the Headquarters of the Army. Pending such regular assignment, the officer commanding the brigade or division is at liberty to detail for temporary duty, in any or each of these several capacities, some officer of his command. But he is not authorized, and hereby is expressly forbidden, to put any civilian, or person not amenable to the Articles of War, on such duty. Any future transgression of this rule will be treated as a disobedience of orders, and dealt with accordingly.

The utmost which is conceded by law and regulation, to any general officer, is the power to select, among the officers of his command, the regularly authorized Aides-de-Camp, to whose services he is entitled, in numbers not to exceed, and of grade no higher, than are designated in section 3 of the act approved July 29, 1861.

But as to the additional Aides-de-Camp authorized by the act approved August 5, 1861, to Major Generals of the *regular* Army, when "commanding forces of the United States *in the field,*" the case is different. Though the power to *recommend* such Aides-de-Camp for appointment, is reserved to these Major Generals, the power of appointing them, when recommended, is exclusively vested in the President, Commander-in-Chief of the Army and Navy, to be exercised or not, at his discretion; and, until regularly appointed by the President, therefore, no officer or civilian, recommended for such appointment, can be placed on duty, or can lawfully exercise any of the functions pertaining to the office.

As a matter of indulgence, and in consideration of the intimate relations which ought to, and must necessarily subsist, between a general officer and his chief of staff, the general officers of volunteers have been allowed to recommend, for appointment, their Assistant Adjutants General. But in this case, as in the others, they will not be permitted to place any one on duty until after he shall have been regularly commissioned or appointed by the President of the United States.

This order establishes no new regulation, but is meant to call attention to long-existing regulations that have been too frequently violated or overlooked, and to put an end to a great abuse.

BY COMMAND OF MAJOR GENERAL McCLELLAN:

L. THOMAS,
Adjutant General.

GENERAL ORDERS,   HEADQUARTERS OF THE ARMY,
ADJUTANT GENERAL'S OFFICE,
No. 13.   *Washington, February* 11, 1862.

The enormous waste, by the officers to whose care they are sent, of the blank forms issued from this office, calls for some prompt correction. With this view, the following regulations have been adopted, and will be strictly enforced:

I..Hereafter all requisitions for books or blanks, supplied from this office, must be addressed, through Regimental and Brigade Headquarters in each Division, to the Assistant Adjutant General at Division Headquarters, who will, himself, from time to time, make general requisitions on this office for the supply of his Division.

II..Every commanding officer of a Company will, henceforth, keep a regular account of all books and blanks received and expended by him for the use of his Company, and make a quarterly return of the same to the Adjutant of his Regiment. These returns will be consolidated with those of the Regimental Headquarters, and forwarded in this shape by the Adjutant, through Brigade Headquarters, to those of the Division. The Assistant Adjutant General at Division Headquarters will make similar returns to this office of the books and blanks received by him for distribution to his Division.

III..Where troops are not brigaded, as sometimes happens with the Cavalry and Artillery, requisitions for books and blanks will be made upon the chiefs of their respective arms in the army to which they are attached, and returns of the same will be made to these officers as though to Division Headquarters; and the Chiefs of Cavalry and Artillery, in such cases, will make requisitions for the books and blanks needed for their commands, and make returns of the same to this office, as prescribed in paragraph II of this order.

IV..The above regulations are meant to apply to regulars as well as to volunteers.

V..Officers on the Recruiting Service, whether of the regular army or the volunteers, will make requisitions for, and quarterly returns of, the books and blanks required by them, on and to their respective Superintendents; and the latter will be governed, in their turn, by what is laid down in paragraph III for the Chiefs of Cavalry and Artillery.

VI..For the regiments of volunteers, organizing or organized, in the several States, and which are still under the direction of their Governors, application must be made to the Adjutant Generals of the States, respectively, and the latter will be supplied from this office on proper requisitions made by them, specifying the number of each kind wanted, and the number of each actually on hand. Quarterly returns must, in such case, also be made to this office, showing the number of each kind of book and blank on hand at date of last return rendered : the number of each kind since received, and the number issued to each regiment, with date of issue. And when the regiments are ordered out of the State, a statement of all the books and blanks distributed to each should be forwarded, by the Adjutant General of the State, to the Headquarters of the Army to which the regiment is ordered, for file at the Headquarters of the Division to which it is assigned.

VII..To each regiment will be allowed the following books, viz:

35 Regulations: 30 Target Practice ;
35 Tactics ;   35 Outpost Duty.
30 Bayonet Exercise ;

VIII..The following will be considered a six-months' supply of blanks and blank books for a regiment : 1 Guard Report Book ; 1 Consolidated Morning Report Book ; 10 Company Morning Report Books ; 100 Consolidated Morning Reports : 2 Lists of Rolls, Returns, &c., to be made out by Company Commanders ; 6 Field and Staff Muster Rolls ; 18 Field and Staff Muster and Pay Rolls ; 6 Muster Rolls of Hospital ; 18 Muster and Pay Rolls, Hospital ; 60 Company Muster Rolls ; 180 Company Muster and Pay Rolls ; 12 Regimental

Returns; 60 Company Monthly Returns; 20 Returns of Men joined Company; 6 Quarterly Regimental Returns of Deceased Soldiers; 30 Quarterly Company Returns of Deceased Soldiers; 2 Annual Returns of Casualties; 40 Descriptive Lists; 100 Non-commissioned Officers' Warrants.

BY COMMAND OF MAJOR GENERAL McCLELLAN:

L. THOMAS,

Adjutant General.

GENERAL ORDERS,   HEADQUARTERS OF THE ARMY,
ADJUTANT GENERAL'S OFFICE,
No. 14.   *Washington, February* 14, 1862.

o   o   o   o   o   o   o

II..The Secretary of War directs that the rations of prisoners held in the rebel States shall be commuted for and during the period of their imprisonment; the commutation to be rated at cost price.

III..Commanders of Military Departments will forward to the Adjutant General estimates of the ordnance and ordnance stores which will be required during the succeeding quarter for the troops under their command. The estimates will be based on true economy and call only for what is essential to the efficiency of the troops. Hereafter, all requisitions for ordnance and ordnance stores required by Regiments, or Companies, serving under the orders of a Department Commander, will be sent *in duplicate* to the said commander, who will order the issue of such part of the requisition as he may judge proper, from the stores which will be placed at his disposal on his own estimate. He will forward the duplicate of each requisition, with his action upon it indorsed, to the Adjutant General. As it may not be practicable to supply immediately all the articles required by each Department Commander, notice will be given, after the receipt of the estimates, what proportion can be supplied, and whence it can be drawn, and the requisitions for troops must be apportioned accordingly.

BY COMMAND OF MAJOR GENERAL McCLELLAN:

L. THOMAS,

Adjutant General.

GENERAL ORDERS, }   HEADQUARTERS OF THE ARMY,
No. 17.   ADJUTANT GENERAL'S OFFICE,
Washington, February 20, 1862.

I..Paragraph II, of "General Orders" No. 102 from the Headquarters of the Army, dated November 25, 1861, directing the transfer of Volunteers, held as prisoners by the enemy, to skeleton regiments, is hereby revoked.

   o   o   o   o   o   o   o   o

BY COMMAND OF MAJOR GENERAL McCLELLAN :

L. THOMAS,
Adjutant General.

GENERAL ORDERS, }   HEADQUARTERS OF THE ARMY,
No. 18.   ADJUTANT'S GENERAL'S OFFICE,
Washington, February 21, 1862.

The following Orders have been received from the War Department :

I..The Governors of States are legally the authorities for raising Volunteer regiments and commissioning their officers. Accordingly, no independent organizations, as such, will be hereafter recognized in the United States service. Copies of the Rolls of Muster into service will be sent as soon as practicable to the Governors of the States to which they belong by the commanders of all brigades, regiments, or corps heretofore recognized as independent of State organizations ; and all vacancies of commissions in such regiments and corps will be hereafter filled by the respective Governors according to law. Wherever a regiment is composed of companies from different States, it will be considered as belonging to the State from which the greatest number of companies was furnished for that regiment.

II..Paragraph 1121 of the Revised Regulations for the Army, of 1861, is amended by adding as follows : In special cases of hard service or exposure, the Quartermaster General may authorize the ration of grain to be increased not more than three pounds, upon a report recommending it by the Chief Quartermaster serving in a Military Department, or with an Army in the field.

III..It has been brought to the notice of the Secretary of War that officers of the Volunteer forces frequently correspond directly with the authorities of the States in which their regiments were raised, and thus procure supplies of clothing and other stores in excess of the Regulation allowance. All requisitions should be made as pointed out in the Regulations, upon the Chief Quartermaster of the Department or Army corps, who will transmit them, through the regular official cannel, to the officer in charge of the depot from which the supplies are to be drawn. All clothing provided heretofore by State authorities and not yet issued, will be turned over to the officers of the United States Quartermaster's Department, who will, as far as possible, issue supplies provided by the States to the troops of the same respectively. The allowance of clothing, &c., which is prescribed in the Army Regulations should never be exceeded, except in urgent cases; and when exceeded, the circumstances making such extra issues necessary should be distinctly and fully set forth on the requisitions, to enable the proper officer to act upon them understandingly. The articles of clothing issued to troops are charged against each man, and must be paid for on final settlement of his pay accounts.

BY COMMAND OF MAJOR GENERAL McCLELLAN :

L. THOMAS,
Adjutant General.

GENERAL ORDERS,	HEADQUARTERS OF THE ARMY,
No. 23.	ADJUTANT GENERAL'S OFFICE,
	Washington, March 3, 1862.

II..By direction of the Secretary of War, the following addition is made to paragraph 9, page 10, Revised Regulations for the Army : Except commissions issued by the President to officers of Volunteer Regiments, which will be considered the same as if issued by the Governors of States.

III..In order to guard against the loss of valuable letters mailed by soldiers in the various Camps, the following order is given, on the recommendation of the Post Office Department : The Commander of each Regiment or Brigade will appoint a trustworthy agent to receive all letters from soldiers containing valuable enclosures. Each letter must be prepaid by postage stamps, together with the registering fee of five cents. A failure to register valuable letters increases the danger of their loss. It will be the duty of the agent to deliver the letters intrusted to him at a convenient post office daily, or as often as mails are forwarded therefrom. He will, with the lett.rs, deliver duplicate lists of the same, giving the names of the writers, and the address upon the letters ; one of which lists, with the registering fee, will be retained by the postmaster. The other copy, signed by the postmaster or registering clerk, will be returned to the agent, as his voucher for the faithful execution of his office.

By command of Major General McClellan :

L. THOMAS,
Adjutant General.

GENERAL ORDERS,   WAR DEPARTMENT,
                    ADJUTANT GENERAL'S OFFICE,
No. 27.   *Washington, March* 21, 1862.

The following Acts and Resolution of Congress are published for the information and government of all concerned :

I..AN ACT to make an additional Article of War.

Be it enacted by the Senate and House of Representatives of the United States of America in Congress assembled, That hereafter the following shall be promulgated as an additional Article of War for the government of the Army of the United States, and shall be obeyed and observed as such :

Article —. All officers or persons in the military or naval service of the United States are prohibited from employing any of the forces under their respective commands for the purpose of returning fugitives from service or labor, who may have escaped from any persons to whom such service or labor is claimed to be due, and any officer who shall be found guilty by a court martial of violating this article shall be dismissed from the service.

Sec. 2. *And be it further enacted,* That this act shall take effect from and after its passage.

Approved March 13, 1862.

12

II..AN ACT to provide for the appointment of sutlers in the volunteer service, and
to define their duties.

*Be it enacted by the Senate and House of Representatives of the United States
of America in Congress assembled,* That the inspector generals of the army
shall constitute a board of officers, whose duty it shall be to prepare,
immediately after the passage of this act, a list or schedule of the following articles which may be sold by sutlers to the officers and soldiers
of the volunteer service, to wit: Apples, dried apples, oranges, figs,
lemons, butter, cheese, milk, sirup, molasses, raisins, candles, crackers,
wallets, brooms, comforters, boots, pocket looking-glasses, pins, gloves,
leather, tin washbasins, shirt buttons, horn and brass buttons, newspapers, books, tobacco, cigars, pipes, matches, blacking, blacking
brushes, clothes brushes, tooth brushes, hair brushes, coarse and fine
combs, emery, crocus, pocket handkerchiefs, stationery, armor oil,
sweet oil, rotten stone, razor strops, razors, shaving soap, soap, sus-
penders, scissors, shoestrings, needles, thread, knives, pencils, and
Bristol brick. Said list or schedule shall be subject, from time to time,
to such revision and change as, in the judgment of the said board, the
good of the service may require : *Provided, always,* That no intoxicating
liquors shall at any time be contained therein, or the sale of such
liquors be in any way authorized by said board. A copy of said list or
schedule, and of any subsequent change therein, together with a copy
of this act, shall be, without delay, furnished by said board to the
commanding officer of each brigade and of each regiment not attached
to any brigade in the volunteer service, and also to the Adjutant General
of the army.

SEC. 2. *And be it further enacted,* That immediately upon the receipt
from said board of said list or schedule and copy of this act by the
commanding officer of any such brigade, the acting brigadier general,
surgeon, quartermaster, and commissary of said brigade shall constitute
a board of officers whose duty it shall be to affix to each article in said
list or schedule a price for said brigade, which shall be by them forthwith reported to the commanding officer of the division, if any, to
which said brigade is attached, for his approval, with or without
modification, and who shall, after such approval, report the same to
the inspector generals, and the same, if not disapproved by them, shall

be the price not exceeding which said articles may be sold to the officers and soldiers in said brigade. Whenever any brigade shall not be attached to a division, said prices shall then be reported directly to the inspector generals, and if approved by them shall be the price fixed for such brigade as aforesaid ; and whenever any regiment shall be unattached to any brigade, the acting colonel, lieutenant colonel, major, and captains thereof shall constitute the board of officers by whom the price of said articles shall be fixed for said regiment in the same manner as is herein provided for an unattached brigade. The prices so fixed may be changed by said boards respectively from 'time to time, not oftener than once in thirty days, but all changes therein shall be reported in like manner and for the same purpose as when originally fixed.

Sec. 3. *And be it further enacted*, That it shall be the duty of the commanding officer of each brigade, immediately upon receipt of a copy of said list or schedule and copy of this act, as herein provided, to cause one sutler for each regiment in his brigade to be selected by the commissioned officers of such regiment, which selection shall be by him reported to the Adjutant General of the army ; the person so selected shall be sole sutler of said regiment. And the commanding officer of each unattached regiment shall, in like manner, cause a selection of a sutler to be made for said regiment, who shall be sole sutler of said regiment. Any vacancy in the office of sutler from any cause shall be filled in the same way as an original appointment.

Sec. 4. *And be it further enacted*, That the sutlers chosen in the manner provided in the preceding section shall be allowed a lien only upon the pay of the 'officers, non-commissioned officers, and privates of the regiment for which he has been chosen, or those stationed at the post to which he has been appointed, and for no greater sum than one-sixth of the monthly pay of each officer, non-commissioned officer, or private, for articles sold during each month ; and the amount of one-sixth or less than one-sixth of the pay of such officer, non-commissioned officer, or private, so sold to him by the sutler, shall be charged on the pay-rolls of such officer, non-commissioned officer, or private, and deducted from his pay, and paid over by the paymaster to the sutler of the regiment or military post, as the case may be : *Provided*, That if any paymaster in the service of the United States shall allow or pay any greater sum to any sutler than that hereby authorized to be retained from the pay of the officers, non-commissioned officers, musicians, and privates, for articles sold by any sutler during any one month, then the amount so allowed or paid by the paymaster shall be charged against the said paymaster and deducted from his pay and returned to the officer, non-commissioned officer, musician, or private, against whom the amount was originally charged. And any captain or lieutenant commanding a company who may certify any pay-roll bearing a charge in favor of the sutler against any officer, non-commissioned officer, musician, or private, larger or greater than one-sixth of the monthly pay of such officer, non-commissioned officer, musician, or private, shall be punished at the discretion of a court-martial : *Provided, however.* That sutlers shall be allowed to sell only the articles designated in the list or schedule provided in this act, and none others, and at prices not exceeding those affixed to said articles, as herein provided : *And provided, further*, That the sutlers shall have no legal claim upon any officer, non-commissioned officer, musician, or private, to an amount exceeding one-sixth of his pay for articles sold during any month. He shall keep said list or schedule, together with a copy of this act, fairly written or printed, posted up in some conspicuous part of the place where he makes said sales, and where the same can be easily read by any person to whom he makes said sales.

Sec. 5. *And be it further enacted*, That it shall be the duty of the inspector generals to cause the place of sale and articles kept for that purpose, by said sutlers, to be inspected from time to time, once in fifteen days at least, by some competent officer, specially detailed for that duty, and such changes in said place, or in the quality and character of the articles mentioned in said list or schedule so kept, as shall be required by said officer shall be conformed to by each sutler And such officer shall report each inspection to the inspector generals.

Sec. 6. *And be it further enacted*, That no person shall be permitted to act as sutler unless appointed according to the provisions of this act ; nor shall any person be sutler for more than one regiment ; nor shall any sutler farm out or underlet the business of sutling or the privileges granted to him by his appointment ; nor shall any officer of the army receive from any sutler any money or other presents ; nor be interested in any way in the stock, trade, or business of any sutler ; and any officer receiving such presents, or being thus interested, directly or indirectly, shall be punished at the discretion of a court-martial. No sutler shall sell to an enlisted man on credit to a sum exceeding one-fourth of his monthly pay within the same month ; nor shall the regimental quartermasters allow the use of army wagons for sutlers' purposes ; nor shall the quartermasters' conveyances be used for the transportation of sutlers' supplies.

SEC. 7. *And be it further enacted*, That any sutler who shall violate any of the provisions of this act shall, by the colonel, with the consent of the council of administration, be dismissed from the service, and be ineligible to a reappointment as sutler in the service of the United States.

Approved March 19, 1862.

III..A RESOLUTION to authorize the Secretary of War to accept moneys appropriated by any State for the payment of its volunteers, and to apply the same as directed by such State.

Resolved by the Senate and House of Representatives of the United States of America in Congress assembled, That if any State, during the present rebellion, shall make any appropriation to pay the volunteers of that State, the Secretary of War is hereby authorized to accept the same, and cause it to be applied, by the Paymaster General, to the payments designated by the legislative acts making the appropriation in the same manner as if appropriated by act of Congress ; and also to make any regulations that may be necessary for the disbursement and proper application of such funds to the specific purpose for which they may be appropriated by the several States.

Approved March 19, 1862.

BY ORDER OF THE SECRETARY OF WAR :

L. THOMAS,
Adjutant General.

GENERAL ORDERS,   WAR DEPARTMENT,
                   ADJUTANT GENERAL'S OFFICE,
No. 28.   *Washington, March 22, 1862.*

○   ○   ○   ○   ○   ○   ○   ○

II..No troops in the United States service will hereafter pass through the city of New York without reporting to the United States military authorities intrusted with the duty of providing subsistence and transportation in that city. Reports must be made and information obtained at the office, No. 79 White street.

III..His Excellency the Governor of New York has decided upon the following prices to be charged to the non-commissioned officers and privates of the several regiments from that State, now in the field, for articles of clothing heretofore furnished them by the State. The said prices have been fixed from the average cost of the several articles :

For each infantry overcoat... $8 63
   "   "   jacket... 5 43
   "   "   trowsers...................................... 3 50
   "   fatigue cap 85
   "   pair of shoes, (pegged) 1 20
   "   "   shoes, (sewed)........................ 1 98
   "   "   drawers 57
   "   "   socks 24
   "   shirt..................................... 88
   "   blanket.................................. 1 95

BY ORDER OF THE SECRETARY OF WAR :

L. THOMAS,
Adjutant General

GENERAL ORDERS,   WAR DEPARTMENT,
                  ADJUTANT GENERAL'S OFFICE,
No. 29.   *Washington, March 22, 1862.*

In the changes recently made in the boundaries of Department commands, it may happen that troops belonging to one Department may either be in, or may unavoidably pass into, another. In such a case, the troops so situated will continue under the command of the General under whose orders they may have been operating. But it is expected that they will be withdrawn as soon as the position they may occupy comes within the control of the proper Commander of the Department.

BY ORDER OF THE SECRETARY OF WAR :

L. THOMAS,
Adjutant General.

GENERAL ORDERS,	WAR DEPARTMENT,
	ADJUTANT GENERAL'S OFFICE,
No. 30.	*Washington, March* 24, 1862.

I..The very great carelessness shown by many detached officers, in keeping this office advised of their movements and address, makes it necessary to recall, in a particular manner, to the attention of every officer of the Army, paragraphs 176, 188, and 468, of the General Regulations, by which all officers on *detached service* and *leave of absence*, are required to make *monthly* reports of their address, as well as of *every change* in their *address*, to this office, and also to their post and regimental commanders.

II..The attention of officers commanding regiments, both volunteer and regular, and of all commanders of Military Departments, separate armies, detached army corps, divisions, and brigades, is once more directed to the subject of returns, and to the absolute necessity of promptly furnishing this office, within the first three days of every month, with an exact return of the forces under their command.

III..The commanding officers of all Military Departments and troops in the field are also reminded that, by General Orders, No. 85, of October 1, 1861, they are required to furnish this office with tri-monthly field returns of their commands, on the 10th, 20th, and last days of each month.

IV..The exceeding importance, at this moment, of the information derived from the above reports and returns—information which can in no other way be obtained—obliges the Secretary of War to reiterate the existing orders on the subject, and to notify all commanding officers that these orders must in future be more punctually obeyed. To this end, he directs that General Orders, No. 74, of September 10, 1861,

2

be republished to the troops, by their Corps, Division, and Brigade Commanders, and urges upon all commanding officers the necessity of giving to this subject their own earnest and unceasing attention.

V...Justice to enlisted men who are separated from their companies, requires that they should have with them Descriptive Rolls showing the pay due them, their clothing accounts, and everything which would be required in settling with the Government, should they be discharged. Without such papers the men cannot receive the pay due them. The especial attention of company commanders is directed to this subject.

VI..The enlisted men on extra duty in the several bureaux, offices, and hospitals, and at the different headquarters, in this city, instead of being paid on separate vouchers, as heretofore, will be mustered together in detachments, under the direction of their respective chiefs. The rolls may be made monthly, so as to constitute consolidated vouchers for each disbursing officer whose duty it may be to pay the men, and will be receipted after the manner of ordinary muster and pay rolls, at the time payment is made.

BY ORDER OF THE SECRETARY OF WAR:

L. THOMAS,
Adjutant General.

GENERAL ORDERS, }   WAR DEPARTMENT,
                       ADJUTANT GENERAL'S OFFICE,
No. 32. }   *Washington, April* 2, 1862.

The following regulations are published for the information of all concerned:

ADDITIONAL PARAGRAPHS ON THE SUBJECT OF PRISONERS OF WAR.

(Vide paragraphs 745 to 747, Revised Regulations for the Army, 1861.)

1. A General commanding in the field, or a Department, will make arrangements for the safe-keeping and reasonable comfort of his prisoners.

2. For this purpose he will place them under a guard already on duty, or detach a guard for the special service.

3. The General will give no order exchanging prisoners, or releasing them, except under instructions from the Secretary of War.

4. In emergencies admitting of no delay, the General will act upon his own authority, and give any order in relation to his prisoners the public interest might require, promptly reporting his proceedings to the War Department through the Adjutant General.

5. In time of war, a Commissary General of Prisoners will be announced, whose general duties will be those of an Inspector.

6. A General Depôt for Prisoners will be designated by the Secretary of War, which shall be under the command of the Commissary General of Prisoners, with a body of troops as a guard under his orders. The Depôt shall be the headquarters of the Commissary General, to which communications may be sent.

7. Generals commanding Departments, or in the field, may, at their discretion, send their prisoners to the General Depôt—furnishing proper rolls with them, showing when and where captured, &c.; after which their charge of them will cease.

8. The Commissary General of Prisoners is empowered to visit places at which prisoners may be held, and will recommend to the General, whose guards are resposible for them, whatever modification in their treatment may seem to him proper or necessary, and report the same to the War Department.

9. Generals sending prisoners to the depôts, or to special localities, will furnish the Commissary General of Prisoners with lists or rolls of all prisoners so sent, which the Commissary General of Prisoners will cause to be entered in a proper book, showing the name and designation of each prisoner, the time and place when and where taken. Any special information of importance will be added from time to time in a column of remarks. When disposed of, by exchange or otherwise, the fact, and the authority for it, and the name of the person for whom exchanged, should be noted in this record.

10. The Commissary General of Prisoners shall have authority to call for such reports from officers in command of guards over prisoners as may be necessary for the proper discharge of his own duties.

11. He will make reports monthly, or oftener, if required, to the

Adjutant General, showing where and in what numbers prisoners are held, and be in readiness at all times to answer specific questions as to persons.

12. The duties of the Commissary General of prisoners do not extend to prisoners of State.

BY ORDER OF THE SECRETARY OF WAR:

L. THOMAS,
Adjutant General.

GENERAL ORDERS,   WAR DEPARTMENT,
ADJUTANT GENERAL'S OFFICE,
No. 33.   *Washington, April 3,* 1862.

    ⚬   ⚬   ⚬   ⚬   ⚬   ⚬   ⚬

II..In order to secure, as far as possible, the decent interment of those who have fallen, or may fall, in battle, it is made the duty of Commanding Generals to lay off lots of ground in some suitable spot near every battle field, so soon as it may be in their power, and to cause the remains of those killed to be interred, with head-boards to the graves bearing numbers, and, where practicable, the names of the persons buried in them. A register of each burial ground will be preserved, in which will be noted the marks corresponding with the head-boards.

III..The recruiting Service for Volunteers will be discontinued in every State from this date. The officers detached on Volunteer Recruiting Service will join their regiments without delay, taking with them the parties and recruits at their respective stations. The Superintendents of Volunteer Recruiting Service will disband their parties and close their offices, after having taken the necessary steps to carry out these orders. The public property belonging to the Volunteer Recruiting Service will be sold to the best advantage possible, and the proceeds credited to the fund for collecting, drilling, and organizing volunteers.

BY ORDER OF THE SECRETARY OF WAR:

L. THOMAS,
Adjutant General.

GENERAL ORDERS,   WAR DEPARTMENT,

                           ADJUTANT GENERAL'S OFFICE,

No. 36.   *Washington, April* 7, 1862.

1..The General Hospitals are under the direction of the Surgeon General. Orders not involving expense of transportation may be given by him to transfer Medical Officers or Hospital Stewards from one General Hospital to another, as he may deem best for the service.

2..The Chief Medical Officer, to whom the charge of all the General Hospitals in a city may be intrusted, will cause certificates of disability to be made out for such men as, in his judgment, should be discharged. He will be responsible that the certificates are given for good cause, and that they are made in proper form, giving such medical description of the cases, with the degree of disability, as may enable the Pension Office to decide on any claim to pension which may be based upon them. The certificates of disability will be signed by the Chief Medical Officer and forwarded by him to the Military Commander in the city, who shall have authority to order the discharge and dispose of the case according to existing regulations.

3..The final statements, and all the discharge papers, will be made out under the supervision of the Military Commander, and signed by him. Where the men are provided with their descriptive rolls there will be no delay in discharging them after their certificates of disability are acted on. But if they have no descriptive rolls, application will be made to the Company Commander for the proper discharge papers, and the men may be maintained at the hospital a reasonable time while awaiting them, to avoid their being turned off without means of support. The discharge will, in all cases, bear the date when the papers are actually furnished the soldier. (See note.)

4..When a man is received in any hospital without his descriptive roll, the fact will be immediately reported by the Medical Officer in charge to the Military Commander, who will at once call on the Company Commander, in the name of the Secretary of War, promptly to furnish the military history of the man, and his clothing, money, and other accounts with the government.

5..When too long a delay would arise in discharging the man because of the remote station of his company, application will be made

by the Medical Officer to the Adjutant General for such account of the
man as his records will furnish. To this partial descriptive roll the
Medical Officer will add the period for which pay is due the man since
his entry into the hospital. The man will then be discharged and
receive the pay and travelling allowances thus shown to be due him,
leaving the balance due him on account of clothing, retained pay, &c.,
for settlement in such manner as may hereafter be determined. (See
notes)

6..The Military Commander's duties, in reference to all troops and
enlisted men who happen to come within the limits of his command,
will be precisely those of a commanding officer of a military post.

7..It is made the duty of each Military Commander to correct, as
far as may be in his power, the evils and irregularities arising from the
peculiar state of the service at this time, by collecting stragglers and
sending them forward to their proper stations, or discharging them
on certificates of disability, if, on examination by the Chief Medical
Officer, they be found unfit for the service.

8..The Military Commander in each city will have control of such
guards as may be furnished to preserve discipline and good order at
the several military hospitals. He will advise the Adjutant General
of the Army what number of companies will be required for such
guards. He will cause them to be properly posted, relieved, and in-
structed.

9..Whenever the Chief Medical Officer shall report a number of
patients as fit to join their regiments, the Military Commander will
give the necessary orders to have them forwarded in good order and
under suitable conduct.

10..The Chief Medical Officer in each city is authorized to employ
as cooks, nurses, and attendants, any convalescent, wounded, or feeble
men who can perform such duties, instead of giving them discharges.

11...All officers and enlisted men of volunteers who are on parole
not to serve against the rebels, will be considered on leave of absence,
until notified of their exchange or discharge. They will immediately

report their address to the Governors of their States, who will be duly informed from this office as to their exchange or discharge.

12.. The duties of Military Commander, as above defined, will devolve. *in the District of Columbia*, on the Military Governor ; *in the city of Baltimore*, on the Commander of the Middle Department; *in the city of Philadelphia*, on Lieutenant Colonel H. Brooks, 2d Artillery, hereby assigned to that station ; *in the city of New York*, and the military posts in that vicinity, on Brevet Brigadier General H. Brown, Colonel 5th United States Artillery.

BY ORDER OF THE SECRETARY OF WAR :

L. THOMAS,
Adjutant General.

NOTE TO PAR. 3 :

The first sentence of this paragraph is modified to read as follows :

The final statements, and all the discharge papers, will be made out under the supervision of the Military Commander, and signed by him, when the soldier is not in a United States hospital, or under the charge of a United States surgeon. But if he is under a United States surgeon or in a United States hospital, the surgeon will, in either case, make out and sign the discharge and final statements, after the Military Commander has indorsed the authority to discharge the soldier upon the usual discharge and certificates of disability.

ADJUTANT GENERAL'S OFFICE,
August 26, 1862.

NOTE TO PAR. 5 :

" In cases where too long a delay would arise in discharging a man because of the remote station of his company," and when no descriptive list or partial descriptive list can be obtained from this office, the men referred to will be discharged under this order, and an order given them on the Quartermaster's Department for transportation to their homes. This order will be signed by the same officer who signs the discharge. The Quartermaster's Department will furnish transportation to such men, upon the presentation of this order, requiring them also to show their discharge.

BY ORDER OF MAJOR GENERAL HALLECK :

E. D. TOWNSEND,
Assistant Adjutant General.

———

NOTE 2d TO PAR. 5 :

The sentence, "To this partial descriptive roll the Medical Officer will add the period for which pay is due the man since his entry into the hospital," will be understood to give him pay *on this final statement* from the muster *next preceding* his entry into the hospital until the date of his discharge.

———

GENERAL ORDERS, }   WAR DEPARTMENT,
                   ADJUTANT GENERAL'S OFFICE,
No. 37. }   *Washington, April 8, 1862.*

The following Resolution of Congress is published for the information of all concerned :

A RESOLUTION to authorize the President to assign the command of troops in the same field or department to officers of the same grade, without regard to seniority.

Resolved by the Senate and House of Representatives of the United States of America in Congress assembled, That whenever military operations may require the presence of two or more officers of the same grade in the same field or department, the President may assign the command of the forces in such field or department, without regard to seniority of rank.

Approved April 4, 1862.

BY ORDER OF THE SECRETARY OF WAR :

L. THOMAS.
Adjutant General.

———

GENERAL ORDERS, }   WAR DEPARTMENT,
                   ADJUTANT GENERAL'S OFFICE,
No. 38. }   *Washington, April 8, 1862.*

Colonel *Anson Stager*, Assistant Quartermaster, has been appointed

Military Superintendent of Telegraph Lines throughout the United States.

Commanding Officers in the military service will, upon the requisition of Colonel Stager, or of his Assistants, give such aid as may be necessary in the construction, repair, and protection of military telegraph lines; and will furnish to the employees connected with those lines, transportation, rations in kind, fuel, lights, stationery, and shelter, such as are allowed to other government employees.

By ORDER OF THE SECRETARY OF WAR:

L. THOMAS,

Adjutant General.

GENERAL ORDERS, }   WAR DEPARTMENT,
                     ADJUTANT GENERAL'S OFFICE,

No. 40 }   *Washington, April* 15, 1862.

The Secretary of War has observed, with some surprise, that the commanders of one or two military departments, conceiving themselves empowered to do so, have undertaken to accept the resignations of, and otherwise discharge from the service of the United States, officers commissioned or appointed by the President, in the volunteer staff of the Army.

All such discharges are irregular, and, unless confirmed by the President, void of effect. None but the President can discharge an officer appointed by himself. And, as he has not delegated this power to any General, no General must attempt to exercise it.

By ORDER OF THE SECRETARY OF WAR:

L. THOMAS,

Adjutant General.

GENERAL ORDERS, }   WAR DEPARTMENT,
                     ADJUTANT GENERAL'S OFFICE,

No. 41. }   *Washington, April* 16, 1862.

I...All agents appointed by the Governor of a State under its laws, to obtain from its volunteer soldiers assignments of pay for the benefit of their families, will be recognized as such by Paymasters, who will afford them all necessary facilities for that purpose, so far as is consistent with the public service.

26

II..Transportation to soldiers on sick-leave may be furnished and the cost stopped from their pay in the same manner as other stoppages are made. Necessary transportation furnished to soldiers on sick-leave by the authorities of any State to which such soldiers belong will be deducted from their pay and refunded to the State by the Paymaster, whose warrant for making the stoppage will be the certificate of the proper agent of the State, accompanied by the receipt of the soldier for the transportation. Where several soldiers of different companies are concerned, separate accounts will be made for each company.

BY ORDER OF THE SECRETARY OF WAR:

L. THOMAS,
Adjutant General.

GENERAL ORDERS, } WAR DEPARTMENT,
ADJUTANT GENERAL'S OFFICE,
No. 42. *Washington, April* 18, 1862.

o   o   o   o   o   o   o   o

IV..The attention of officers empowered by law to assemble General Courts Martial is directed to the Regulations, paragraphs 896 and 897, relative to forwarding the proceedings of such Courts, with their action indorsed on each case, and a copy of the order promulgating the proceedings, promptly, to the Judge Advocate of the Army, at Washington. Much embarrassment is occasioned to the War Department by failure to comply with these Regulations, which must be at once remedied wherever they have been neglected.

BY ORDER OF THE SECRETARY OF WAR:

L. THOMAS,
Adjutant General.

GENERAL ORDERS, } WAR DEPARTMENT,
ADJUTANT GENERAL'S OFFICE,
No. 43. *Washington, April* 19, 1862.

The following act of Congress is published for the information of all concerned:

AN ACT to reorganize and increase the efficiency of the medical department of the Army.

Be it enacted by the Senate and House of Representatives of the United States of America in Congress assembled, That there shall be added to the present medical corps of the army ten surgeons and ten assistant surgeons, to be promoted and appointed under existing laws; twenty medical cadets, and as many hospital stewards as the Surgeon General may consider necessary for the public service, and that their pay and that of all hospital stewards in the volunteer as well as the regular service shall be thirty dollars per month, to be computed from the passage of this act. And all medical cadets in the service shall, in addition to their pay, receive one ration per day, either in kind or commutation.

SEC. 2. *And be it further enacted*, That the Surgeon General to be appointed under this act shall have the rank, pay, and emoluments of a brigadier general. There shall be one assistant surgeon general and one medical inspector general of hospitals, each with the rank, pay, and emoluments of a colonel of cavalry, and the medical inspector general shall have, under the direction of the Surgeon General, the supervision of all that relates to the sanitary condition of the army, whether in transports, quarters, or camps, and of the hygiene, police, discipline, and efficiency of field and general hospitals, under such regulations as may hereafter be established.

SEC. 8. *And be it further enacted*, That there shall be eight medical inspectors, with the rank, pay, and emoluments each of a lieutenant colonel of cavalry, and who shall be charged with the duty of inspecting the sanitary condition of transports, quarters, and camps, of field and general hospitals, and who shall report to the medical inspector general, under such regulations as may be hereafter established, all circumstances relating to the sanitary condition and wants of troops and of hospitals, and to the skill, efficiency, and good conduct of the officers and attendants connected with the medical department.

SEC. 4. *And be it further enacted*, That the Surgeon General, the assistant surgeon general, medical inspector general, and medical inspectors, shall, immediately after the passage of this act, be appointed by the President, by and with the advice and consent of the Senate, by selection from the medical corps of the army, or from the surgeons in the volunteer service, without regard to their rank when so selected, but with sole regard to qualifications.

SEC. 5. *And be it further enacted*, That medical purveyors shall be charged, under the direction of the Surgeon General, with the selection

28

and purchase of all medical supplies, including new standard preparations, and of all books, instruments, hospital stores, furniture, and other articles required for the sick and wounded of the army. In all cases of emergency they may provide such additional accommodations for the sick and wounded of the army, and may transport such medical supplies as circumstances may render necessary, under such regulations as may hereafter be established, and shall make prompt and immediate issues upon all special requisitions made upon them under such circumstances by medical officers; and the special requisitions shall consist simply of a list of the articles required, the qualities required, dated, and signed by the medical officers requiring them.

SEC. 6. *And be it further enacted*, That whenever the inspector general, or any one of the medical inspectors, shall report an officer of the medical corps as disqualified, by age or otherwise, for promotion to a higher grade, or unfitted for the performance of his professional duties, he shall be reported by the Surgeon General, for examination, to a medical board, as provided by the seventeenth section of the act approved August third, eighteen hundred and sixty-one.

SEC. 7. *And be it further enacted*, That the provisions of this act shall continue and be in force during the existence of the present rebellion and no longer: *Provided, however*, That, when this act shall expire, all officers who shall have been promoted from the medical staff of the army under this act shall retain their respective rank in the army, with such promotion as they would have been entitled to.

Approved April 16, 1862.

BY ORDER OF THE SECRETARY OF WAR:

L. THOMAS,
Adjutant General.

GENERAL ORDERS, }
No. 46. }

WAR DEPARTMENT,
ADJUTANT GENERAL'S OFFICE,
Washington, April 23, 1862.

II..Surgeons from civil life who tender their services for the sick and wounded in the field, under the invitation of the Secretary of

War, will each be allowed, while so employed, the use of a public horse, a tent, the necessary servants, and the privilege of purchasing subsistence stores from the Commissary Department.

III..The attention of Commanders of Armies, Departments, Divisions, and detached Brigades, by whom paragraph 448, General Regulations, has been neglected, is specially directed to its requirement concerning forwarding copies of all their orders to the Adjutant General's Office.

By order of the Secretary of War:

L. THOMAS,
Adjutant General.

GENERAL ORDERS,   WAR DEPARTMENT,
ADJUTANT GENERAL's OFFICE,
No. 47.   *Washington, April* 26, 1862.

When the care of sick and wounded soldiers is assumed by the States from which they come, the Subsistence Department will commute their ration at twenty-five cents.

By order of the Secretary of War:

L. THOMAS,
Adjutant General.

GENERAL ORDERS,   WAR DEPARTMENT,
ADJUTANT GENERAL'S OFFICE,
No. 48.   *Washington, April* 28, 1862.

11..Applications for transportation for the removal of sick men, for nurses, and for supplies for the sick, will be made hereafter to the Surgeon General The Surgeon General is also authorized to give passes at his discretion for private physicians, nurses, and friends of sick and wounded soldiers to attend and visit them.

By order of the Secretary of War:

L THOMAS,
Adjutant General.

GENERAL ORDERS. No. 49.

WAR DEPARTMENT,
ADJUTANT GENERAL'S OFFICE,
Washington, May 1, 1862.

Upon requisitions made by Commanders of Armies in the field, authority will be given by the War Department to the Governors of the respective States to recruit Regiments now in service.

BY ORDER OF THE SECRETARY OF WAR :

L. THOMAS,
Adjutant General.

GENERAL ORDERS, No. 51.

WAR DEPARTMENT,
ADJUTANT GENERAL'S OFFICE,
Washington, May 10, 1862.

I..Commanders of Departments will designate some officer in each city or town where there is a General Hospital, to perform the functions assigned to military commanders in " General Orders," No. 36.

II..When rations are commuted at twenty-five cents, under the provisions of " General Orders," No. 47, the physician in charge of the State hospitals will enter on their descriptive lists the dates between which the men have been subsisted.

III..When transportation is furnished to soldiers on sick leave, under paragraph II of " General Orders," No. 41, the Officers or Surgeons of General Hospitals, who grant the furloughs, will note the cost of such transportation on the descriptive lists of the men.   Quartermasters will not hereafter pay bills for such transportation to the States.

IV..Paragraph II of " General Orders," No. 102, dated November 25, 1861, having been revoked, the officers and men transferred to skeleton regiments under its operation will be reassigned to their original regiments as fast as vacancies occur.   Remarks will be made opposite their names on the Muster Rolls, showing the dates of their capture, transfer from, and retransfer to, their respective companies ; and also whether they are exchanged or still on parole.

BY ORDER OF THE SECRETARY OF WAR :

L. THOMAS,
Adjutant General.

GENERAL ORDERS,   WAR DEPARTMENT,
          ADJUTANT GENERAL'S OFFICE,
No. 52.   *Washington, May 14, 1862.*

I..All officers absent on leave will proceed without delay to join their regiments, except those on parole and those recently exchanged. Officers who are too sick to travel, will immediately report the length of time they have been absent, and forward to this office a medical description of their case by a medical officer of the Army, or, where that cannot be obtained, by a competent physician.

II..The names of officers and men taken prisoners by the enemy must not be dropped from the muster rolls, but will be placed at the foot of the list of names, in their respective companies, until they are exchanged or discharged.

BY ORDER OF THE SECRETARY OF WAR :

          L. THOMAS,
           Adjutant General.

GENERAL ORDERS,   WAR DEPARTMENT,
          ADJUTANT GENERAL'S OFFICE,
No. 53.   *Washington, May 16, 1862.*

The following acts of Congress are published for the information of all concerned :

 o o o o o o o o

II..AN ACT to facilitate the discharge of enlisted men for physical disability.

Be it enacted by the Senate and House of Representatives of the United States of America in Congress assembled, That the medical inspector general, or any medical inspector, is hereby authorized and empowered to discharge from the service of the United States any soldier or enlisted man, with the consent of such soldier or enlisted man, in the permanent hospitals, laboring under any physical disability which makes it disadvantageous to the service that he be retained therein, and the certificate, in writing, of such inspector general or medical inspector, setting forth the existence and nature of such physical disability, shall be sufficient evidence of such discharge : *Provided, however,* That every such certificate shall appear on its face to have been founded on personal inspection of the soldier so discharged, and shall specifically describe the nature and origin of such disability; and that such discharge shall be without prejudice to the right of such soldier or enlisted man to the pay due him at the date thereof, and report the same to the Adjutant General and the Surgeon General.

Approved May 14, 1862.

By order of the Secretary of War :

L. THOMAS,
Adjutant General.

GENERAL ORDERS, }   WAR DEPARTMENT,
                       ADJUTANT GENERAL'S OFFICE.
No. 54. }   *Washington, May* 17, 1862.

o   o   o   o   o   o   c

II..The Commissary General of Prisoners and commanding officers having charge of prisoners of war, will, as soon as practicable, forward to this office lists of the prisoners, showing their rank, regiment, where captured, date of confinement, and where confined. Similar lists will be furnished of new detachments as often as they may arrive at their several places of confinement.

o   o   o   o   o   o   o

By order of the Secretary of War:

L. THOMAS,
Adjutant General.

GENERAL ORDERS, }   WAR DEPARTMENT,
                       ADJUTANT GENERAL'S OFFICE,
No. 55. }   *Washington, May* 24, 1862.

I..The following Act of Congress is published for the information of all concerned:

AN ACT to authorize the appointment of medical storekeepers and chaplains of hospitals.

Be it enacted by the Senate and House of Representatives of the United States of America in Congress assembled, That the Secretary of War be authorized to add to the medical department of the army, medical storekeepers, not exceeding six in number, who shall have the pay and emolum nts of military storekeepers in the quartermaster's department, who shall be skilled apothecaries or druggists, who shall give the bond and security required by existing laws for military storekeepers in the quartermaster's department, and who shall be stationed at such points as the necessities of the army may require: *Provided*, That the provisions of this act shall remain in force only during the continuance of the present rebellion.

SEC. 2. *And be it further enacted*, That the President of the United States is hereby authorized to appoint, if he shall deem it necessary, a chaplain for each permanent hospital, whose pay, with that of chaplains of hospitals heretofore appointed by him, shall be the same as that of regimental chaplains in the volunteer force; and who shall be subject to such rules in relation to leave of absence from duty as are prescribed for commissioned officers of the army.

Approved May 20. 1862.

II...The following are the Regulations which will govern the appointment of medical storekeepers under the first section of the foregoing act of Congress:

1. A board of not less than three medical officers will be assembled by the Secretary of War to examine such applicants as may, by him, be authorized to appear before it.

2. Candidates, to be eligible to examination, shall be not less than 25 years, or more than 40 years of age; shall possess sufficient physical ability to perform their duties satisfactorily; and shall present with their applications satisfactory evidence of good moral character.

3. Candidates will be required to pass a satisfactory examination in the ordinary branches of a good English education, in pharmacy and materia medica; and to give proof that they possess the requisite business qualifications for the position.

4. The board will report to the Secretary of War the relative merit of the candidates examined, and they will receive appointments accordingly.

5. When appointed, each medical storekeeper will be required to

give a bond in the amount of $40,000, before he shall be allowed to enter on the performance of his duties.

BY ORDER OF THE SECRETARY OF WAR:

L. THOMAS,
Adjutant General.

GENERAL ORDERS,   WAR DEPARTMENT,
                   ADJUTANT GENERAL'S OFFICE,
No. 56.   *Washington, May 29,* 1862.

Officers serving in the Quartermaster's Department will issue to signal parties of the Army serving in their vicinity, such supplies as may be necessary for their proper equipment, on the requisition of the officer in charge of such parties.

Rations will be issued to signal parties in like manner by officers of the Commissary Department.

BY ORDER OF THE SECRETARY OF WAR:

L. THOMAS,
Adjutant General.

GENERAL ORDERS,   WAR DEPARTMENT,
                   ADJUTANT GENERAL'S OFFICE,
No. 58.   *Washington, June 4,* 1862.

The following act of Congress is published for the information and government of all concerned:

AN ACT to prevent and punish fraud on the part of officers intrusted with making of contracts for the government.

Be it enacted by the Senate and House of Representatives of the United States of America in Congress assembled, That it shall be the duty of the Secretary of War, of the Secretary of the Navy, and of the Secretary of the Interior, immediately after the passage of this act, to cause and require every contract made by them, severally, on behalf of the government, or by their officers under them appointed to make such contracts, to be reduced to writing, and signed by the contracting parties with their names at the end thereof, a copy of which shall be filed by the officer making and signing the said contract in the "Returns Office" of the Department of the Interior (hereinafter established for that purpose) as soon after the contract is made as possible, and within thirty days, together with all bids, offers, and proposals to him made by persons to obtain the same, as also a copy of any advertisement he may have published inviting bids, offers, or proposals for the same; all the said copies and papers in relation to each contract to be attached together by a ribbon and seal, and numbered in regular order numerically, according to the number of papers composing the whole return.

SEC. 2. *And be it further enacted*, That it shall be the further duty of the said officer, before making his return according to the first section of this act, to affix to the same his affidavit in the following form, sworn to before some magistrate having authority to administer oaths: "I do solemnly swear (or affirm) that the copy of contract hereto annexed is an exact copy of a contract made by me personally with ———— ————; that I made the same fairly, without any benefit or advantage to myself, or allowing any such benefit or advantage corruptly to the said ———— ————, or any other person; and that the papers accompanying include all those relating to the said contract, as required by the statute in such case made and provided." And any officer convicted of falsely and corruptly swearing to such affidavit, shall be subject to all the pains and penalties now by law inflicted for wilful and corrupt perjury.

SEC. 3. *And be it further enacted*, That any officer making contracts, as aforesaid, and failing or neglecting to make returns of the same, according to the provisions of this act, unless from unavoidable accident and not within his control, shall be deemed, in every case of such failure or neglect, to be guilty of a misdemeanor, and, on conviction thereof, shall be punished by a fine of not less than one hundred dollars, nor more than five hundred dollars, and be imprisoned for not more than six months, at the discretion of the court trying the same.

SEC. 4. *And be it further enacted*, That it shall be the duty of the Secretary of the Interior, immediately after the passage of this act, to provide a fit and proper apartment in his department, to be called the "Returns Office," within which to file the returns required by this act to be filed, and to appoint a clerk to attend to the same, who shall be

entitled to an annual salary of twelve hundred dollars, and whose
duty it shall be to file all returns made to said office, so that the same
may be of easy access, filing all returns made by the same officer in
the same place, and numbering them as they are made in numerical
order. He shall also provide and keep an index book, with the names
of the contracting parties, and the number of each and every contract
opposite to the said names; and he shall submit the said index book
and returns to any person desiring to inspect the same; and he shall
also furnish copies of said returns to any person paying for said copies
to said clerk at the rate of five cents for every one hundred words, to
which said copies certificates shall be appended in every case by the
clerk making the same, attesting their correctness, and that each copy
so certified is a full and complete copy of said return; which return,
so certified under the seal of the Department, shall be evidence in all
prosecutions under this act.

Sec. 5. *And be it further enacted*, That it shall be the duty of the
Secretary of War, of the Secretary of the Navy, and of the Secretary
of the Interior, immediately after the passage of this act, to furnish
each and every officer severally appointed by them with authority to
make contracts on behalf of the government, with a printed letter of
instructions, setting forth the duties of such officer under this act, and
also to furnish therewith forms, printed in blank, of contracts to be
made, and the affidavit of returns required to be affixed thereto, so
that all the instruments may be as nearly uniform as possible.

Approved June 2, 1862.

By order of the Secretary of War:

L. THOMAS,
Adjutant General.

GENERAL ORDERS,	WAR DEPARTMENT,
	ADJUTANT GENERAL'S OFFICE,
No. 60.	*Washington, June 6, 1862.*

I..The Volunteer Recruiting Service, discontinued by "General
Orders," No. 33, of April 3, 1862, is hereby restored according to the

principles laid down in "General Orders," Nos. 105, of 1861, and 3, of 1862. Invalid or disabled officers, necessarily absent from their regiments, will be detailed for this duty whenever they are able to perform it.

II..A large number of volunteers are absent from their regiments who are now fit for duty. To enable them to return, the Governors of States are authorized to give them certificates or passes which will entitle them to transportation to the station of the nearest U. S. Mustering Office or Quartermaster, who will pay the cost of transportation on such certificate or pass, and provide transportation for the soldier to his regiment or station.

III..All Captains of Companies are hereby required to report quarterly to the Chief of Ordnance the kind of arms in use by their companies, their opinion of the suitableness of the arm, the general extent of service, and the number requiring repairs since the previous report.

IV..The principle being recognized that Medical Officers should not be held as prisoners of war, it is hereby directed that all Medical Officers so held by the United States shall be immediately and unconditionally discharged.

BY ORDER OF THE SECRETARY OF WAR:

L. THOMAS,
Adjutant General.

GENERAL ORDERS, }
No. 61. }

WAR DEPARTMENT,
ADJUTANT GENERAL'S OFFICE,
Washington, June 7, 1862.

The great number of officers absent from their regiments without sufficient cause is a serious evil which calls for immediate correction. By paragraph 177, General Regulations, the power of commanding officers to grant leaves of absence is limited to a "time of peace." In time of war leaves of absence will only be granted by the Secretary of War, except when the certificate of a medical officer shall show, beyond doubt, that a change of location " is necessary to save life, or prevent *permanent* disability." (*Paragraph* 186, *General Regulations.*) In such case, the Commander of an Army, a Department, or a District, may grant not exceeding twenty days. At the expiration of that time, *if the officer be not able to travel,* he must make application to the Adjutant General of the Army for an extension, accompanied by the certificate of a medical officer of the army, in the usual form, and that he is not able to travel. If it be not practicable to procure such a certificate, in consequence of there being no army physician in the place where the officer resides, the certificate of a citizen physician, *attested by a civil magistrate,* may be substituted.

All officers of the Regulars and Volunteers, except those on parole, now absent from duty with leave, will be considered "absent without leave," (*paragraph* 1326, *General Regulations,*) unless they are found at their posts within fifteen days from the date of this order, or are authorized by orders from the Adjutant General to be absent, which orders will in all cases be based on a certificate as above described, and must be exhibited to the paymaster before payment is made them.

All invalid and wounded officers who are able to travel, although their disability may not have been removed (*paragraph* 187, *General Regulations*) will repair, without delay—those from the East to Annapolis, to report to the General Commanding the Camp of Instruction ; those from the West to report to the commanding officer of Camp Chase, Ohio. At those points they will remain until able to proceed to their regiments, or until an examining board may decide adversely on their ability to return to duty within a reasonable time, and orders may be given by the President for their discharge.

Their Excellencies the Governors of States are requested to make known this order, and to contribute to its execution, as may be in their power. Mustering and Recruiting Officers are directed to do the same. Extra copies of the order will be furnished them for distribution.

Failure to comply with the above regulations will be reported to the Adjutant General by Regimental Commanders.

By order of the Secretary of War:

L. THOMAS,
Adjutant General.

GENERAL ORDERS,   WAR DEPARTMENT,
                       ADJUTANT GENERAL'S OFFICE,
No. 64.   *Washington, June* 11, 1862.

I..All property captured by the Army, or seized by any Provost Marshal, or taken up estray, or taken from soldiers marching in the enemy's country, will be turned over to the Chiefs of the Staff Departments to which such property would appertain, on duty with the troops, and will be accounted for by them as captured property, and used for the public service, unless claimed by owners and ordered by the commanding officer to be returned. In such case, the receipts of the owners to whom the property is delivered will be taken therefor. Provost Marshals will make returns to the Adjutant General of all such property and of the disposition made of it, accounting on separate returns for ordnance, quartermaster, subsistence, medical stores, &c., furnishing and procuring the usual invoices and receipts, and charging the officers to whom the property has been delivered, with the same, on the returns.

II..Paragraph 41, Regulations for the Subsistence Department, of April 24, 1862, corresponding with paragraph 1217, Regulations for the Army, is hereby rescinded. The settlement of accounts for the board of soldiers in private hospitals is transferred to the Surgeon General's Department.

BY ORDER OF THE SECRETARY OF WAR :

L. THOMAS,
Adjutant General.

GENERAL ORDERS,   WAR DEPARTMENT,
                       ADJUTANT GENERAL'S OFFICE,
No. 65.   *Washington, June* 12, 1862.

I..Paragraph 1269, Army Regulations, is hereby so modified that Private Physicians, employed as Medical Officers with an Army in the field in time of war, may be allowed a sum not to exceed one hundred and twenty-five dollars per month, besides transportation in kind.

II..The certificates of discharge to be given by the Medical Inspector General, or any Medical Inspector of the Army, under the Act of May 14, 1862, published in "General Orders," No. 53, will be made on the printed forms for Certificates of Disability, prescribed by the Army Regulations. The Inspector giving the discharge will indorse it with his own certificate that it is granted upon his own personal inspection of the soldier, and with the soldier's consent ; and for disability, the nature, degree, and origin of which are correctly described in the within certificate.

III.._Each Medical Director must, under the orders of his Department Commander, regulate the distribution of the sick and wounded to the hospitals within the Military Department to which he belongs. When want of room in such hospitals, or the nature of the wounds or diseases of any invalids, require that detachments shall be sent beyond the limits of their departments, the Surgeon General will designate to the Medical Directors, either by general instructions, or specially by telegraph, to what points they shall be sent. Officers, whose duty it may become to forward such detachments, will take care that no men, except those provided with written passes from their Hospital Surgeon or the Medical Director, shall be allowed to go.

Furloughs will not be given by Captains of Companies or Colonels of Regiments on any pretext whatever. A furlough from such authority will not relieve a soldier from the charge of desertion.

Enlisted men absent from their regiments without proper authority, are in fact *deserters*, and not only forfeit all pay and allowances, but are subject to the penalties awarded by law to such offenders. No plea of sickness, or other cause not *officially* established, and no certificate of a physician in civil life, unless it be approved by some officer acting as a military commander, *will hereafter avail to remove the charge of desertion, or procure arrears of pay*, when a soldier has been mustered as absent from his regiment *without leave.*

By application to the Governors of their States, or to any Military Commander, or United States Mustering Officer in a city, transportation can be procured to their regiments by soldiers who are otherwise able to join them.

Where no Military Commander has been appointed, the senior officer of the Army on duty as Mustering or Recruiting Officer in the place, is hereby authorized and required to act in that capacity until another may be appointed.

Under "General Orders," No. 36, it is the duty of Military Commanders to collect all stragglers and forward them to their regiments. To do this, they must establish camps or depots, under strict military discipline, and maintain sufficient guards to maintain this order. Convalescents in army hospitals will be reported by the surgeons in charge to the Military Commanders, to be kept at their camps or depots until they can be sent to join their regiments. Muster rolls of each detachment will be made out from the best data at hand, the statement of the men being taken in the absence of other information concerning them. A duplicate of each muster roll must be forwarded to the Adjutant General the day the detachment starts.

To avoid confusion and retain necessary control over all soldiers in the United States service, those who are entertained in State or private hospitals must be subject to the nearest Military Commander, and are hereby required to report to him in person as soon as they become convalescent.

Immediately after receipt of this order, each Military Commander will publish, three times, in some newspaper, a brief notice requiring all United States soldiers in that city and the country around, who are not under treatment in a United States hospital, to report themselves to him without delay on penalty of being considered deserters. In cases of serious disability from wounds or sickness, which may prevent obedience to this requirement, the soldier must furnish a certificate of a physician of good standing, describing his case, on which, if satisfactory, the Military Commander may grant a written furlough for not exceeding thirty days, or a discharge on the prescribed form of a certificate of disability, made out strictly according to the Regulations. But no discharges will be given on account of rheumatism, or where there is a prospect of recovery within a reasonable time.

Military Commanders may discharge men, *at their own request*, who exhibit to them satisfactory proof of their being *paroled* prisoners of war. To other paroled men they will give furloughs until notified of their exchange, or discharged the service

Military Commanders will report to the Adjutant General, tri-monthly, the names, companies, regiments, and residences of all the soldiers furloughed or discharged by them ; and forward, at the same time, the certificates of disability in case of discharge.

They will make timely requisitions for the blanks, and such other things as may be necessary for the proper execution of this order.

BY ORDER OF THE SECRETARY OF WAR :

L. THOMAS,
Adjutant General.

GENERAL ORDERS, } WAR DEPARTMENT,
ADJUTANT GENERAL'S OFFICE,
No. 67. } *Washington, June* 17, 1862.

The supervision of Prisoners of War sent by Generals commanding in the field to posts or camps prepared for their reception, is placed entirely under Colonel WILLIAM HOFFMAN, Third Infantry, Commissary General of Prisoners, who is subject only to the orders of the War Department. All matters in relation to prisoners will pass through him.

He will establish regulations for issuing clothing to prisoners, and will direct the manner in which all funds arising from the saving of rations at prison hospitals, or otherwise, shall be accounted for and disbursed by the regular disbursing officers of the Departments, in providing, under existing regulations, such articles as may be absolutely necessary for the welfare of the prisoners.

He will select positions for camps for prisoners, (or prison camps,) and will cause plans and estimates for necessary buildings to be prepared and submitted to the Quartermaster General, upon whose approval they will be erected by the officers of the Quartermaster's Department.

He will, if practicable, visit the several prison camps once a month.

Loyal citizens who may be found among the prisoners of war, confined on false accusations or through mistake, may lay their cases before the Commissary General of Prisoners, who will submit them to the Adjutant General.

The Commissary General is authorized to grant paroles to prisoners, on the recommendation of the Medical Officer attending the prison, in case of extreme illness, but under no other circumstances.

BY ORDER OF THE SECRETARY OF WAR:

L. THOMAS,
Adjutant General.

GENERAL ORDERS,   WAR DEPARTMENT,
                          ADJUTANT GENERAL'S OFFICE,

No. 68.   *Washington, June* 18, 1862.

I..Whenever soldiers are discharged while absent from their companies, the *officers granting the discharge* will furnish them with *final statements* for pay, and *certificates of discharge.* The same officers, including Medical Inspectors, will, *in all cases,* notify the *Adjutant General* and the *commanding officer* of the *company* to which the soldier belongs, of the *date, place,* and *cause* of such discharge. Certificates of disability are never to be given into the hands of the soldier, but are to be forwarded to the Adjutant General, after being completed. (*See paragraphs* 167 *and* 168 *General Regulations.*)

II..The act of February 13, 1862, section 2, published in "General Orders," No. 15, although prohibiting the discharge of minors from the service, does not authorize their enlistment or muster into service, except with the written consent of their parents, masters, or guardians. Such consent must be taken in triplicate, and filed with triplicate copies of the muster-in rolls.

III..Officers now or hereafter detached from their regiments for Signal duty, will report immediately for orders to the Signal Officer of the Army; after which they will not be relieved from such duty, except by orders from the Adjutant General of the Army.

BY ORDER OF THE SECRETARY OF WAR:

                     L THOMAS,
                       Adjutant General.

GENERAL ORDERS,   WAR DEPARTMENT,
                          ADJUTANT GENERAL'S OFFICE,

No. 69.   *Washington, June* 19, 1862.

The following is published for the information and guidance of all concerned, in connexion with the Act of June 2, 1862, promulgated in "General Orders," No. 58:

                     WAR DEPARTMENT,
                       WASHINGTON CITY, D. C.,
                       June 16, 1862.

The Secretary of War is of opinion that the "Act to prevent and punish fraud on the part of officers intrusted with making contracts on the part of government," approved June 2, 1862, applies only to such contracts as, under the laws and regulations in force at the time of its passage, were required to be in writing. The execution of the act, in any other sense, is utterly impracticable, and an attempt otherwise to enforce it, would everywhere instantly arrest the operation of all our forces. It is therefore

Ordered, That all contracts, which by the present regulations are prescribed to be made in writing, shall hereafter be made in quintuplicate, of which four shall be disposed of according to such regulations, and one shall be sent by the officer making and signing the same to the Returns Office of the Department of the Interior, within thirty days after the contract is made, together with all proposals, and a copy of any advertisement published by him touching the same, attached and verified in the manner required by the act above specified. EDWIN M. STANTON,

Secretary of War.

BY ORDER OF THE SECRETARY OF WAR:

L. THOMAS,

Adjutant General.

GENERAL ORDERS, } WAR DEPARTMENT,
ADJUTANT GENERAL'S OFFICE,
No. 70. } *Washington, June* 20, 1862.

The following Act of Congress is published for the information and government of all concerned:

AN ACT providing that the officers of volunteers shall be paid on the pay-rolls of the regiments or companies to which they belong.

Be it enacted by the Senate and House of Representatives of the United States of America in Congress assembled, That company officers of volunteers shall be paid on the muster and pay rolls of their company, party, or detachment, and not otherwise, except when such officer may be on detached service without troops, or on leave of absence.

Approved June 18, 1862.

BY ORDER OF THE SECRETARY OF WAR:

L. THOMAS,

Adjutant General

GENERAL ORDERS,   WAR DEPARTMENT,
ADJUTANT GENERAL'S OFFICE,
No. 71.   *Washington, June* 21, 1862.

In every case of prisoners taken in arms against the United States, who may be tried and sentenced to death, the record of the tribunal before which the trial was had will be forwarded for the action of the President of the United States, without whose orders no such sentence, in such cases, will be executed.

BY ORDER OF THE SECRETARY OF WAR:

L. THOMAS,
Adjutant General.

GENERAL ORDERS,   WAR DEPARTMENT,
ADJUTANT GENERAL'S OFFICE,
No. 72   *Washington, June* 28, 1862.

I.. Whenever *sick* men, *paroled* prisoners, or others, under circumstances entitling them to their descriptive lists and accounts of pay and clothing, &c., *are sent away from their regiments*, or, being already separated from their regiments, are discharged *from any hospital*, or moved from point to point *in a body*, they will be put under charge of a trusty officer or non-commissioned officer—to be selected, if possible, from their own number—who will exercise command over the party and conduct it to its destination. And to this officer or non-commissioned officer *will be confided the descriptive lists of all;* for the safe-keeping of which, until properly turned over with each soldier, he will be held strictly accountable. Detailed instructions, in writing, for his guidance and government during the journey, will, in every case, if possible, be furnished to such officer by his last commander. And should he, himself, be compelled to make any detachments from his party, he will, in each case, observe the same rules.

II.. That paragraph of General Orders, No. 65, of June 12, 1862, which authorizes the discharge, *when requested by them,* of *paroled* prisoners, is hereby rescinded.

III.. *No more furloughs will be granted to paroled prisoners. All furloughs heretofore given to them are hereby revoked;* and all prisoners, now at large

46

on their parole, or who may hereafter be paroled by the rebel authorities, will immediately repair—if belonging to regiments raised in the New England and Middle States, to the Camp of Instruction established near Annapolis, Md. ; if belonging to regiments raised in the States of Virginia, Tennessee, Kentucky, Ohio, Indiana, and Michigan, to Camp Chase, near Columbus, Ohio; if belonging to regiments raised in the States of Illinois, Wisconsin, Minnesota, Iowa, and Missouri, to the Camp near Jefferson Barracks, Mo.,—and report for such duty, compatible with their parole, as may be assigned to them by the officers in command of said camps. *And all, whether officers or soldiers, who fail to comply with this order, within the space of time necessary for them to do so,* will be accounted *deserters* and dealt with accordingly.

The attention of all commanding, mustering, and recruiting officers is particularly directed to this order, and they are required to use their utmost exertions, not only to give it the widest circulation in their neighborhoods, but to see that it is faithfully carried out. And their Excellencies the Governors of the several States are respectfully solicited to lend their efforts to the same end.

IV.–The transportation necessary to a compliance with this order, can, on application, be procured from the Governors of the several States, or from the United States mustering or commanding officers in the various cities within them.

V.–The commanders of the different Camps of Instruction, to which paroled men are sent, will have them organized into companies and battalions, keeping those of the same regiment and of the same State as much together as possible ; and will have correct *muster-rolls* of them made out and forwarded to this office ; and, on the 15th day of every muster month, will furnish a list of them to the company commanders;—from whom, in return, they will procure full and exact *descriptive lists* of each man, and *accounts* of the *pay, clothing, &c.,* due to or from him to the government.

BY ORDER OF THE SECRETARY OF WAR:

L. THOMAS,
Adjutant General.

GENERAL ORDERS,   WAR DEPARTMENT,
                 ADJUTANT GENERAL'S OFFICE,
No. 74.   *Washington, July 7,* 1862.

I.. The following Resolution of Congress is published for the information of all concerned:

A RESOLUTION to encourage Enlistments in the Regular Army and Volunteer forces.

Resolved by the Senate and House of Representatives of the United States of America in Congress assembled, That so much of the ninth section of the act approved August third, eighteen hundred and sixty-one, entitled "An act for the better organization of the military establishment," as abolishes the premium paid for bringing accepted recruits to the rendezvous, be and the same is hereby repealed, and hereafter a premium of two dollars shall be paid to any citizen, non-commissioned officer, or soldier, for such accepted recruit for the regular army [as] he may bring to the rendezvous. And every soldier who hereafter enlists, either in the regular army or the volunteers, for three years, or during the war, may receive his first month's pay in advance, upon the mustering of his company into the service of the United States, or after he shall have been mustered into and joined a regiment already in the service.

Approved June 21, 1862

  ○   ○   ○   ○   ○   ○

III.. For *volunteer recruits,* for *old* regiments, there will be paid a premium of three dollars, and for those entering new regiments a premium of two dollars. The premium may be paid either to the person bringing the recruit, or to the recruit in person, in case he presents himself.

These payments will be made so soon as the recruit has been inspected by the surgeon and mustered into the service.

The amounts will be entered on the Muster-in Roll, opposite the names of the recruits so paid, and charged to the fund for "*collecting, drilling, and organizing volunteers*"

For a voucher, a modified form of that used in the regular service may be used.

IV.. The month's pay in advance for regular and volunteer recruits will be paid under such regulations as the Paymaster General may establish.

V...During the continuance of the existing war, *twenty-five dollars of the one hundred bounty* previously authorized by act of Congress will be paid to every recruit of the regular and volunteer forces.

These payments will be made as follows, viz :

1. To volunteer recruits for the old regiments, when the said recruits are inspected and mustered into the service, and to those of the new regiments when their companies are organized, muster-in rolls made out, and the mustering officer's certificate given thereto. The amounts will be entered on the muster-in rolls, opposite the name of the recruits, respectively, and charged under the head of *"Expenses of Volunteer Recruiting Service."* To this end, an account current separate from that for the fund for "collecting, drilling, and organizing volunteers," will be used, but the "volunteer recruiting fund" will be disbursed by the regularly appointed mustering and disbursing officers.

○   ○   ○   ○   ○   ○   ○   ○

3. Vouchers for payment will be in the form of consolidated receipt rolls.

BY ORDER OF THE SECRETARY OF WAR :

L. THOMAS,
Adjutant General.

We, the undersigned, do hereby acknowledge to have received from Lieut. ————, ———— Regiment of ————, ————, Recruiting Officer, [or from ————, Mustering and Disbursing Officer,] the sums opposite our names, respectively, being in full for amounts due us for procuring and bringing to the rendezvous accepted recruits. Our names are placed opposite the names of recruits so furnished, and we have signed duplicates hereof.

DATE.	No.	NAME OF RECRUIT.	AMOUNT.	NAME OF PERSON PROCUR-ING RECRUITS."	WITNESS.	REMARKS.

I CERTIFY that the above is correct; that the recruits accepted are "effective and able-bodied;" and that, in accepting them, I have been strictly governed by paragraphs 925 and 926 Recruiting Regulations.

————, Lieut. ———— Infantry, Recruiting Officer.

NOTES.—1. Act of February 13, 1833, published in G. O. No. 15, although prohibiting discharge of minors from the service, does not authorize their enlistment or muster into service, except with written consent of parent, guardian, or master.

2. It should be borne in mind that the law provides for the enlistment of "effective, able-bodied" men; and if any officer shall enlist any person contrary to the true intent and meaning of the law, it is further provided that, for every offence, "he shall forfeit and pay the amount of the bounty and clothing which the person so recruited may have received from the public, to be deducted out of the pay and emoluments of such officer."

* In case of volunteer recruits the name of the recruit will appear in this column in case the money was paid to him.

4

GENERAL ORDERS,   WAR DEPARTMENT,
                       ADJUTANT GENERAL'S OFFICE,
    No. 75.   *Washington, July* 8, 1862.

I..In organizing new Regiments of Volunteers, the Governors of States are hereby authorized to appoint, in addition to the Staff officers heretofore authorized, one Second Lieutenant for each Company, who shall be mustered into the service at the commencement of the organization, who shall have authority to muster in recruits as they are enlisted. If any recruit shall be enlisted by such officer, who shall afterwards, on medical inspection, prove to have been obviously unfit for the service at the time of his enlistment, all expenses caused thereby shall be paid by such officer, to be stopped against him from any payment that may be coming to him from the Government thereafter

Any officer, thus appointed and mustered, shall only be entitled to be paid on the muster and pay roll of his company, and should he fail to secure an organized company within such reasonable time as the Governor may designate, his men may be transferred to some other company, his appointment be revoked, and be discharged without pay; unless the Governor shall think proper to give him a position in the consolidated company to which his men have been transferred.

Articles of enlistment, as in the regular army, will be made out in triplicate by such recruiting officers, one copy of which will be sent to the Adjutant General of the State, one to the Adjutant of the Regiment, and one will be kept by the recruiting officer.

Recruits will be sent to the regimental rendezvous at least as often as once a week, where they will be immediately examined by the Surgeon of the Regiment, and, if found unfit for duty by reason of permanent disability, will be discharged from the service forthwith by the Surgeon, who will report such discharges to the Adjutant General of the State, and also to the Adjutant of the Regiment, noting particularly those cases where the disability was obvious at the time of enlistment.

The muster-in rolls of each company will be made out by the Adjutant of the Regiment, from a list to be furnished by the Adjutant General of the State, together with the articles of enlistment furnished him by the recruiting officer, and will note upon it the names of all persons discharged by the Surgeon for permanent disability, designating particularly those cases where the disability was apparent at the time of enlistment.

As soon as the organization of a regiment is completed, it will be carefully inspected by the mustering officer for the State, who will see that at least the minimum number of each company is present; no absentees, except sick in hospital, will be counted. He will also compare the muster-in rolls, and, if found correct, will sign the roll, certifying to the muster of each man at the date of his enlistment.

Mustering officers will report promptly to the Adjutant General of the Army the names of all recruiting Lieutenants mustered into the service by them, under conditional letters of appointment, together with the Regiments to which they belong.

II..Officers will be mustered into the service only on the authority of the Governor of the State to which their regiments belong.

III..Until regiments are organized and their muster rolls completed, they will be under the exclusive control of the Governors of the States, and all requisitions for quartermaster, medical, and ordnance stores, and contracts for subsistence, will, if approved by them, be allowed, and not otherwise.

IV..Where it is desired by the Governors of States, the United States officers of the quartermaster, medical, and ordnance departments may turn over stores to the State authorities, to be issued by them in accordance with the regulations, and accounted for to the proper Bureau of the War Department.

V..Persons travelling under the order of the Governor of a State on business connected with the recruiting service, will be allowed the actual cost of transportation, to be paid by the mustering and disbursing officer on presentation of the account, accompanied by proper vouchers, and the order under which the journey was performed.

By order of the Secretary of War:

L. THOMAS,
Adjutant General.

GENERAL ORDERS,   WAR DEPARTMENT,

                       ADJUTANT GENERAL'S OFFICE,

No. 77.   *Washington, July* 11, 1862.

The following act of Congress is published for the information of all concerned:

AN ACT making appropriations for the support of the Army for the year ending the thirtieth of June, eighteen hundred and sixty-three, and additional appropriations for the year ending thirtieth of June, eighteen hundred and sixty-two, and for other purposes.

Be it enacted by the Senate and House of Representatives of the United States of America in Congress assembled, That the following sums be, and the same are hereby, appropriated, out of any money in the Treasury not otherwise appropriated, for the support of the army for the year ending the thirtieth of June, eighteen hundred and sixty-three.

   o   o   o   o   o   o   o

For pay of volunteers under acts of twenty-second and twenty-fifth of July, eighteen hundred and sixty-one, two hundred and twenty-six millions two hundred and eighty-three thousand two hundred and eighty-two dollars: *Provided,* That the President shall not be authorized to appoint more than forty major generals, nor more than two hundred brigadier generals. And all acts and parts of acts authorizing a greater number of major and brigadier generals than are above provided for are hereby repealed.

   o   o   o   o   o   o   o

For payment of bounty to volunteers, and to the widows and legal heirs of such as may die or be killed in the service of the United States, authorized by the fifth and sixth sections of an act entitled " An act to authorize the employment of volunteers to aid in enforcing the laws and protecting public property," approved July twenty-second, eighteen hundred and sixty-one, twenty millions of dollars, or so much thereof as may be found necessary.

For collecting, organizing, and drilling volunteers, in addition to any sums heretofore appropriated for that purpose, five millions of dollars.

For providing for the comfort of discharged soldiers who may arrive in the principal cities of the United States so disabled by disease or by wounds received in the service as to be unable to proceed to their homes, and for forwarding destitute soldiers to their homes, two millions of dollars, to be applied and expended under the direction of the President of the United States.

    ○   ○   ○   ○   ○   ○   ○   ○

Sec. 2. *And be it further enacted*, That so much of the seventh section of the act approved third March, eighteen hundred and fifty-one, entitled "An act to found a military asylum for the relief and support of invalid and disabled soldiers of the army of the United States," as requires that "all moneys, not exceeding two-thirds of the balance on hand, of the hospital fund and of the post fund of each military station, after deducting the necessary expenses," shall be set apart for the support of the military asylum, be and the same is hereby repealed.

    ○   ○   ○   ○   ○   ○   ○   ○

Sec 4. *And be it further enacted*, That in all cases where recruiting officers have in good faith paid the two dollars for bringing accepted recruits to the rendezvous, before receiving notice of the repeal of the regulation allowing the same, the accounts of such officer shall be allowed in settlement by the Treasury Department.

    ○   ○   ○   ○   ○   ○   ○   ○

Sec. 6. *And be it further enacted*, That section five of the act "to authorize the employment of volunteers to aid in enforcing the laws and protecting public property," approved July twenty-second, eighteen hundred and sixty-one, and section five of the act "to increase the present military establishment of the United States," approved July twenty-nine, eighteen hundred and sixty-one, shall be so construed as to allow twenty-five dollars of the bounty of one hundred dollars therein provided to be paid immediately after enlistment to every soldier of the regular and volunteer forces hereafter enlisted during the continuance of the existing war, and the sum of seven millions five hundred thousand dollars is hereby appropriated for such payment.

Sec. 7. *And be it further enacted*, That all the aides-de-camp appointed by authority of the act approved fifth August, eighteen hundred and sixty-one, entitled "An act supplementary to an act entitled an act to increase the present military establishment of the United States," approved July twenty-nine, eighteen hundred and sixty-one, shall be nominated to the Senate for its advice and consent.

    ○   ○   ○   ○   ○   ○   ○   ○

Sec. 10. *And be it further enacted*, That the Secretary of War be authorized to commute the army ration of coffee and sugar, for the extract of coffee, combined with milk and sugar, to be procured in the same manner and under like restrictions and guarantees as preserved meats, pickles, butter, and desiccated vegetables are procured for the navy, if he shall believe it will be conducive to the health and com-fort of the army, and not more expensive to the Government than the present ration, and if it shall be acceptable to the men.

✿ ✿ ✿ ✿ ✿ ✿ ✿ ✿

By order of the Secretary of War:

E. D. TOWNSEND,

Assistant Adjutant General.

GENERAL ORDERS,   WAR DEPARTMENT,
ADJUTANT GENERAL'S OFFICE,
No. 78.   *Washington, July* 14, 1862.

1..The many evils which arise from giving furloughs to enlisted men, require that the practice shall be discontinued. Hospitals, provided with ample medical attendance, nurses, food, and clothing, are established by the Government, at great expense, not only near the scenes of active military operations, but in many of the Northern States. When it is expedient and advisable, sick and wounded patients may, under the direction of the Surgeon General, be trans-ferred in parties, but not in individual cases, to hospitals at the North; and, as far as practicable, the men will be sent to States in which their regiments were raised, provided United States hospitals have been established there. Such regulations will be adopted at all the hospitals as will permit relatives and friends to visit the patients, and furnish them with comforts, at such hours and in such manner as will not interfere with the discipline of the hospitals and the welfare of the mass of patients. The men will thus be under the fostering care of the Government while unfit for duty; will be in position to be promptly discharged if proper, and, being always under military control, will be returned to their regiments as soon as they are able to resume their duties. The unauthorized removal of soldiers from under the control of the United States authorities, by any agents whatever, subjects them to loss of pay and other penalties of desertion.

II.. At large camps, depots, or posts, where absentees arrive *en route* to their companies, the commanding officers will immediately set apart a particular place where the men may be quartered, in buildings, tents, or huts, as soon as they arrive, and may, *without delay*, receive food and clothing. Parties will be detailed to await at landing places the arrival of such soldiers, and to direct them to their quarters. They will be assigned immediately to temporary companies, composed as far as possible of men from the same regiments or brigades; and each of these companies will be forwarded in a body to the command to which they belong, according to the directions contained in paragraph I of "General Orders," No. 72.

III.. Chaplains appointed by the President for hospitals, will be assigned by the Surgeon General to hospitals in the cities for which they were appointed. Should the breaking up of a hospital leave a chaplain supernumerary in any city, the fact will be immediately reported to the Adjutant General. Chaplains will be subordinate to the hospital surgeons. Leaves of absence will be granted them by the Surgeon General when approved by the Surgeons in charge of their hospitals.

BY ORDER OF THE SECRETARY OF WAR:

L. THOMAS,
Adjutant General.

GENERAL ORDERS,	WAR DEPARTMENT,
	ADJUTANT GENERAL'S OFFICE,
No. 79.	*Washington, July* 15, 1862.

I.. The following Acts of Congress are published for the information of all concerned:

1.. AN ACT making appropriations for the payment of the bounty authorized by the sixth section of an act entitled "An act to authorize the employment of volun_ teers to aid in enforcing the laws and protecting public property," approved July twenty-second, eighteen hundred and sixty-one, and for other purposes.

Be it enacted by the Senate and House of Representatives of the United States of America in Congress assembled, That the following sums be, and the same

are hereby, appropriated, out of any money in the Treasury not otherwise appropriated, for the objects hereinafter expressed, viz :

For payment of the bounty to widows, children, fathers, mothers,
brothers, and sisters of such volunteers as may have died or been
killed, or may die or be killed, in service, authorized by the sixth
section of an act entitled "An act to authorize the employment of
volunteers to aid in enforcing the laws and protecting public property,"
approved July twenty-second, eighteen hundred and sixty-one, five
millions of dollars, or so much thereof as may be found necessary :
Provided, That said bounty shall be paid to the following persons, and
in the order following, and to no other person, to wit : First, to the
widow of such deceased soldier, if there be one. Second, if there be
no widow, then to the children of such deceased soldier, share and
share alike. Third, if such soldier left neither a widow or child or
children, then, and in that case, such bounty shall be paid to the following persons, provided they be residents of the United States, to
wit: First, to his father; or if he shall not be living, or has abandoned
the support of his family, then to the mother of such soldier; and if
there be neither father nor mother as aforesaid, then such bounty shall
be paid to the brothers and sisters of the deceased soldier, resident as
aforesaid.

o   o   o   o   o   o

SEC. 3. *And be it further enacted,* That that part of the sixth section of
the act "to authorize the employment of volunteers to aid in enforcing
the laws and protecting public property," approved July twenty-second,
eighteen hundred and sixty-one, which secured to the widow, if there
be one, and if not, the legal heirs of such volunteer as die or may be
killed in service, in addition to all arrears of pay and allowances, a
bounty of one hundred dollars, shall be held to apply to those persons
who have enlisted in the regular forces since the first day of July, eighteen hundred and sixty-one, or shall enlist in the regular forces during
the year eighteen hundred and sixty-two, and be paid to the heirs
named in this act, and that the bounties herein provided for shall be
paid out of any money appropriated for bounty to volunteers.

Approved July 11, 1862.

2..AN ACT to provide for additional medical officers of the volunteer service.

Be it enacted by the Senate and House of Representatives of the United States of America in Congress assembled, That there shall be appointed by the President, by and with the advice and consent of the Senate, forty surgeons and one hundred and twenty assistant surgeons of volunteers, who shall have the rank, pay, and emoluments of officers of corresponding grades in the regular army : *Provided,* That no one shall be appointed to any position under this act unless he shall previously have been examined by a board of medical officers to be appointed by the Secretary of War, and that vacancies in the grade of surgeon shall be filled by selection from the grade of assistant surgeon on the ground of merit only : *And provided further,* That this act shall continue in force only during the existence of the present rebellion.

SEC 2. *And be it further enacted,* That from and after the passage of this act briga le surgeons shall be known and designated as surgeons of volunteers, and shall be attached to the general medical staff under the direction of the Surgeon General ; and hereafter such appointments for the medical service of the army shall be appointed surgeons of volunteers.

SEC. 3. *And be it further enacted,* That instead of "one assistant surgeon," as provided by the second section of the act of July 22, 1861, each regiment of volunteers in the service of the United States shall have two assistant surgeons

Approved July 2, 1862.

II..Under the provisions of the foregoing act, approved July 2, 1862, the Brigade Surgeons already appointed are transferred, according to their present rank, to the Corps of Volunteer Surgeons, which will accordingly consist of those officers and of the forty provided for by the act.

The Surgeon General will appoint a Board to examine such persons as may be authorized by the Secretary of War to present themselves before it as candidates for the forty vacancies in the grade of Surgeon and one hundred and twenty in that of Assistant Surgeon.

Applications for the appointments will be made to the Adjutant

General of the Army, in the handwriting of the applicant, accompanied by one or more testimonials from respectable persons in regard to moral character.

The Board of Examiners will determine whether the candidate be fit for the position of Surgeon or Assistant Surgeon ; but no one under thirty years of age will be appointed to the former grade, or under twenty-one years to the latter grade.

After all the vacancies have been filled in the manner here prescribed, future examinations will be for the grade of Assistant Surgeon only, and vacancies which may happen in the grade of Surgeon will be filled by the appointment of Assistant Surgeons who shall have shown themselves worthy of promotion by a faithful performance of duty and general good conduct.

BY ORDER OF THE SECRETARY OF WAR :

L. THOMAS,
Adjutant General.

GENERAL ORDERS,   WAR DEPARTMENT,
                           ADJUTANT GENERAL'S OFFICE,
No. 80.   *Washington, July* 16, 1862.

The following Act of Congress is published for the information and government of all concerned :

AN ACT to prescribe an oath of office, and for other purposes.

Be it enacted by the Senate and House of Representatives of the United States of America in Congress assembled, That hereafter every person elected or appointed to any office of honor or profit under the Government of the United States, either in the civil, military, or naval departments of the public service, excepting the President of the United States, shall, before entering upon the duties of such office, and before being entitled to any of the salary or other emoluments thereof, take and subscribe to the following oath or affirmation : "I, A. B., do solemnly swear (or affirm) that I have never voluntarily borne arms against the United States since I have been a citizen thereof ; that I have voluntarily given no aid, countenance, counsel, or encouragement to persons engaged in armed hostility thereto ; that I have neither sought nor accepted nor attempted to exercise the functions of any office whatever under any authority or pretended authority in hostility to the United States ; that I have not yielded a voluntary support to any pretended government, authority, power, or constitution within the United States, hostile or inimical thereto. And I do further swear (or affirm) that, to the best of my knowledge and ability, I will support and defend the Constitution of the United States against all enemies, foreign and domestic ; that I will bear true faith and allegiance to the same ; that I take this obligation freely, without any mental reservation or purpose of evasion ; and that I will well and faithfully discharge the duties of the office on which I am about to enter, so help me God ;'' which said oath, so taken and signed, shall be preserved among the files of the Court, House of Congress, or Department to which the said office may appertain. And any person who shall falsely take the said oath shall be guilty of perjury, and on conviction, in addition to the penalties now prescribed for that offence, shall be deprived of his office and rendered incapable forever after of holding any office or place under the United States.

Approved July 2, 1862.

BY ORDER OF THE SECRETARY OF WAR :

L. THOMAS,
Adjutant General.

GENERAL ORDERS,	WAR DEPARTMENT,
	ADJUTANT GENERAL'S OFFICE,
No. 82.	*Washington, July* 21, 1862.

The following order has been received from the President of the United States :

Representations have been made to the President by the Ministers of various foreign powers in amity with the United States, that subjects of such powers have, during the present insurrection, been obliged or required by military authorities to take an oath of general or quali- fied allegiance to this Government. It is the duty of all aliens residing in the United States to submit to and obey the laws, and respect the authority of the Government. For any proceeding or conduct inconsistent with this obligation, and subversive of that authority, they may rightfully be subjected to military restraints when this may be necessary. But they cannot be required to take an oath of allegiance to this Government, because it conflicts with the duty they owe to their own sovereigns. All such obligations heretofore taken are, therefore, remitted and annulled. Military Commanders will abstain from imposing similar obligations in future, and will, in lieu thereof, adopt such other restraints of the character indicated as they shall find necessary, convenient, and effectual, for the public safety. It is further directed that whenever any order shall be made affecting the personal liberty of an alien, reports of the same, and of the causes thereof, shall be made to the War Department, for the consideration of the Department of State.

BY ORDER OF THE SECRETARY OF WAR:

L. THOMAS,
Adjutant General.

GENERAL ORDERS,
No. 83.

WAR DEPARTMENT,
ADJUTANT GENERAL'S OFFICE,
Washington, July 22, 1862.

In organizing new Regiments of Volunteers, the subsistence of the recruits, prior to the completion of the organization, will be chargeable against the appropriation " for collecting, drilling, and organizing volunteers." After the organization of the regiments is completed, and they have been inspected by the mustering officer for the State, subsistence will be provided by the Subsistence Department.

BY ORDER OF THE SECRETARY OF WAR :

L. THOMAS,
Adjutant General

GENERAL ORDERS,   WAR DEPARTMENT,
                ADJUTANT GENERAL'S OFFICE,
No. 85.   *Washington, July 23, 1862.*

The following order is published for the information of the Army :

WAR DEPARTMENT,
Washington City, D. C., July 22, 1862.

ORDER *in respect to clothing for sick and wounded soldiers.*

The following is a Joint Resolution of Congress, approved 12th July, 1862 :

JOINT RESOLUTION authorizing the Secretary of War to furnish extra clothing to sick, wounded, and other soldiers.

Resolved by the Senate and House of Representatives of the United States of America in Congress assembled, That the Secretary of War be authorized to furnish extra clothing to all sick, wounded, and other soldiers who may have lost the same by casualties of war, under such rules and regulations as the Department may prescribe, during the existence of the present rebellion.

In pursuance of the foregoing resolution, it is ordered, that the Quartermaster's Department shall issue, upon the requisition of the Medical Officer in charge of any hospital or depot of sick and wounded soldiers, such regulation clothing, necessary to their health and comfort, as may be requisite to replace that lost by them from the casualties of war. The necessity of the issue to be certified by the Surgeon, and the requisition to be approved by the Medical Director or Medical Inspector of the station. Such issue to be gratuitous and not charged to the soldier.

The Quartermaster General will cause blank requisitions to be furnished to the officers of the various hospitals upon their application.

EDWIN M. STANTON,
Secretary of War.

BY ORDER OF THE SECRETARY OF WAR:

L. THOMAS,
Adjutant General.

GENERAL ORDERS,   WAR DEPARTMENT,
                 ADJUTANT GENERAL'S OFFICE,
   No. 86.   *Washington*, July 23, 1862.

1.._Descriptive lists_ and *accounts* of the *pay*, *clothing*, &c., of soldiers, will never, where it can be avoided, be given into their own hands. Such papers should be intrusted only to the officer or non-commissioned officer in charge of the party with which they are.

II..Except in such cases as that of an Ordnance Sergeant, specially assigned to duty at a post where there are no troops, and where he cannot be regularly mustered, *no soldier must be paid on a mere descriptive list and account of pay and clothing*, but only upon the muster and pay roll of his company, detachment, or party, or on that of a general hospital, if he ·be there sick or on duty. *No payments will, therefore, be made to enlisted men on furlough.*

III..The giving *in duplicate*, by any officer of the Army, of *certificates of discharge*, or *final statements*, is peremptorily forbidden; (see paragraph 165 of the Revised Regulations) Not even if such papers are lost or destroyed, is any officer of the Army authorized to replace them.

IV..The proper course to be pursued in such cases will be found indicated in paragraph 1341 of the Revised Regulations, and is substantially as follows:

Application for payment in these cases must be made *through the Paymaster General of the Army*, to the Second Comptroller of the Treasury. The application must be accompanied by the soldier's statement, under oath, that his final statements and certificate of discharge are lost, destroyed, or have never been received by him; that he has made diligent search or application for them; that they cannot be recovered or obtained; and that he has not received pay on them, nor assigned them to any other person.

All the circumstances of the case must be fully set forth in the affidavit, and this again must be accompanied by all the evidence in corroboration of his statement, which the soldier can procure.

On receipt of this, the Second Comptroller will audit the account, and, if satisfied with the evidence, will order payment to the soldier of the amount found justly due to him.

V..The attention of all officers of the army—and particularly of all company, regimental, and post commanders, surgeons in charge of general hospitals and paymasters, and of all soldiers discharged from the service, who, from the want of their final statements and certificates of discharge, are unable to procure a settlement of their accounts with the Government—is specially directed to this order.

BY ORDER OF THE SECRETARY OF WAR:

L. THOMAS,
Adjutant General.

GENERAL ORDERS, } WAR DEPARTMENT,
ADJUTANT GENERAL'S OFFICE,
No. 88. } *Washington, July 25,* 1862.

I..The recruiting detail for each volunteer regiment in the field will hereafter consist of two commissioned officers from the regiment and *one non-commissioned officer or private from each company.* Paragraph III of " General Orders," No. 105, of 1861, is amended accordingly. Regimental commanders will at once select the additional men herein authorized; and the order for detail will, as before, be given by the Commanders of Departments or Corps d'Armeé.

2..One commissioned officer of the detail will remain constantly at the general recruiting depot to receive the recruits when sent from the rendezvous, and to exercise care and control over them after their arrival until they are ordered to their regiments.

3..*Recruits for regiments now in the field will be permitted to select any company of the regiment they may prefer.* Should the company thus selected be full when they join it, they will be allowed to select another.

4..*All men who desire, singly or by squads, to join any particular regiment or company* in the field, are hereby authorized to present themselves to any recruiting officer, when they will be enrolled and forwarded at once to the general depot for the State or district, there to be duly mustered, and to receive the bounty allowed by law. In such cases enlistment papers and descriptive lists will be forwarded as directed in " General Orders," No. 105, of 1861, from this office.

BY ORDER OF THE SECRETARY OF WAR:

L THOMAS,
Adjutant General.

64

GENERAL ORDERS, } WAR DEPARTMENT,
ADJUTANT GENERAL'S OFFICE,
No. 90. } *Washington, July 26, 1862.*

I..The principle being recognized that Chaplains should not be held as prisoners of war, it is hereby ordered that all Chaplains so held by the United States shall be immediately and unconditionally discharged.

o   o   o   o   o   o   o

BY ORDER OF THE SECRETARY OF WAR :

L. THOMAS,
Adjutant General.

___

GENERAL ORDERS, } WAR DEPARTMENT,
ADJUTANT GENERAL'S OFFICE,
No. 91. } *Washington, July 29, 1862.*

The following Resolutions, Acts, and Extracts from Acts, of Congress, are published for the information of all concerned:

o   o   o   o   o   o   o

I..PUBLIC RESOLUTION—No. 43.

A RESOLUTION to provide for the presentation of "medals of honor" to the enlisted men of the army and volunteer forces who have distinguished or may distinguish themselves in battle during the present rebellion.

Resolved by the Senate and House of Representatives of the United States of America in Congress assembled, That the President of the United States be, and he is hereby, authorized to cause two thousand "medals of honor" to be prepared, with suitable emblematic devices, and to direct that the same be presented, in the name of Congress, to such non_ commissioned officers and privates as shall most distinguish themselves by their gallantry in action, and other soldier-like qualities, during the present insurrection. And that the sum of ten thousand dollars be, and the same is hereby, appropriated out of any money in the Treasury not otherwise appropriated, for the purpose of carrying this Resolution into effect.

Approved July 12, 1862.

II..PUBLIC—No. 137.

AN ACT to grant pensions.

Be it enacted by the Senate and House of Representatives of the United States of America in Congress assembled, That if any officer, non-commissioned

officer, musician, or private of the army, including regulars, volunteers, and militia, or any officer, warrant or petty officer, musician,
seaman, ordinary seaman, flotillaman, marine, clerk, landsman, pilot,
or other person in the navy or marine corps, has been, since the fourth
day of March, eighteen hundred and sixty-one, or shall hereafter be,
disabled by reason of any wound received or disease contracted while
in the service of the United States, and in the line of duty, he shall,
upon making due proof of the fact according to such forms and regulations as are or may be provided by or in pursuance of law, be placed
upon the list of invalid pensions of the United States, and be entitled
to receive, for the highest rate of disability, such pension as is hereinafter provided in such cases, and for an inferior disability an amount
proportionate to the highest disability, to commence as hereinafter provided, and continue during the existence of such disability. The pension for a total disability for officers, non-commissioned officers, musicians, and privates employed in the military service of the United
States, whether regulars, volunteers, or militia, and in the marine corps,
shall be as follows, viz: Lieutenant colonel, and all officers of a higher
rank, thirty dollars per month; major, twenty-five dollars per month;
captain, twenty dollars per month; first lieutenant, seventeen dollars
per month; second lieutenant, fifteen dollars per month; and non-commissioned officers, musicians, and privates, eight dollars per month.
The pension for total disability for officers, warrant or petty officers,
and others employed in the naval service of the United States, shall be
as follows, viz: Captain, commander, surgeon, paymaster, and chief
engineer, respectively, ranking with commander by law, lieutenant
commanding, and master commanding, thirty dollars per month; lieutenant, surgeon, paymaster, and chief engineer, respectively, ranking
with lieutenant by law, and passed assistant surgeon, twenty-five
dollars per month; professor of mathematics, master, assistant surgeon,
assistant paymaster, and chaplain, twenty dollars per month; first
assistant engineers and pilots, fifteen dollars per month; passed midshipman, midshipman, captain's and paymaster's clerk, second and
third assistant engineer, master's mate, and all warrant officers, ten
dollars per month; all petty officers, and all other persons before named
employed in the naval service, eight dollars per month; and all com-

missioned officers of either service, shall receive such and only such pension as herein provided for the rank in which they hold commissions.

SEC. 2. *And be it further enacted*, That if any officer or other person named in the first section of this act, has died since the fourth day of March, eighteen hundred and sixty-one, or shall hereafter die, by reason of any wound received or disease contracted while in the service of the United States, and in the line of duty, his widow, or, if there be no widow, his child or children under sixteen years of age, shall be entitled to receive the same pension as the husband or father would have been entitled to had he been totally disabled, to commence from the death of the husband or father, and to continue to the widow during her widowhood, or to the child or children until they severally attain the age of sixteen years and no longer.

SEC. 3. *And be it further enacted*, That where any officer or other person named in the first section of this act shall have died subsequently to the fourth day of March, eighteen hundred and sixty-one, or shall hereafter die, by reason of any wound received or disease contracted while in the service of the United States, and in the line of duty, and has not left or shall not leave a widow nor legitimate child, but has left or shall leave a mother who was dependent upon him for support, in whole or in part, the mother shall be entitled to receive the same pension as such officer or other person would have been entitled to had he been totally disabled; which pension shall commence from the death of the officer or other person dying as aforesaid: *Provided, however*, That if such mother shall herself be in receipt of a pension as a widow, in virtue of the provisions of the second section of this act, in that case no pension or allowance shall be granted to her on account of her son, unless she gives up the other pension or allowance: *And provided, further*, That the pension given to a mother on account of her son shall terminate on her remarriage; *And provided, further*, That nothing herein shall be so construed as to entitle the mother of an officer or other person dying, as aforesaid, to more than one pension at the same time under the provisions of this act.

SEC. 4. *And be it further enacted*, That where any officer or other person named in the first section of this act shall have died subsequently to the fourth day of March, eighteen hundred and sixty-one, or shall hereafter die, by reason of any wound received or disease contracted while in the service of the United States and in the line of duty, and has not left or shall not leave a widow, nor legitimate child, nor mother, but has left or may leave an orphan sister or sisters, under sixteen years of age, who were dependent upon him for support, in whole or in part, such sister or sisters shall be entitled to receive the same pension as such officer or other person would have been entitled to had he been totally disabled; which pension to said orphan shall commence from the death of the officer or other person dying as aforesaid, and shall continue to the said orphans until they severally arrive at the age of sixteen years, and no longer: *Provided, however,* That nothing herein shall be so construed as to entitle said orphans to more than one pension at the same time, under the provisions of this act: *And provided, further,* That no moneys shall be paid to the widow, or children, or any heirs of any deceased soldier on account of bounty, back pay, or pension, who have in any way been engaged in or who have aided or abetted the existing rebellion in the United States; but the right of such disloyal widow or children, heir or heirs of such soldier, shall be vested in the loyal heir or heirs of the deceased, if any there be.

Sec. 5. *And be it further enacted,* That pensions which may be granted, in pursuance of the provisions of this act, to persons who may have been, or shall be, employed in the military or naval service of the United States, shall commence on the day of the discharge of such persons in all cases in which the application for such provisions is filed within one year after the date of said discharge; and in cases in which the application is not filed during said year, pensions granted to persons employed as aforesaid shall commence on the day of the filing of the application.

Sec. 6. *And be it further enacted,* That the fees of agents and attorneys, for making out and causing to be executed the papers necessary to establish a claim for a pension, bounty, and other allowance, before the Pension Office under this act, shall not exceed the following rates:

For making out and causing to be duly executed a declaration by the applicant, with the necessary affidavits, and forwarding the same to the Pension Office, with the requisite correspondence, five dollars. In cases wherein additional testimony is required by the Commissioner of Pensions, for each affidavit so required and executed and forwarded, (except the affidavits of surgeons, for which such agents and attorneys shall not be entitled to any fees,) one dollar and fifty cents.

Sec. 7. *And be it further enacted*, That any agent or attorney who shall, directly or indirectly, demand or receive any greater compensation for his services under this act than is prescribed in the preceding section of this act, or who shall contract or agree to prosecute any claim for a pension, bounty, or other allowance under this act, on the condition that he shall receive a per centum upon, or any portion of the amount of, such claim, or who shall wrongfully withhold from a pensioner or other claimant the whole or any part of the pension or claim allowed and due to such pensioner or claimant, shall be deemed guilty of a high misdemeanor, and upon conviction thereof shall, for every such offence, be fined not exceeding three hundred dollars, or imprisoned at hard labor not exceeding two years, or both, according to the circumstances and aggravations of the offence.

Sec. 8. *And be it further enacted*, That the Commissioner of Pensions be, and he is hereby, empowered to appoint, at his discretion, civil surgeons to make the biennial examinations of pensioners which are or may be required to be made by law, and to examine applicants for invalid pensions, where he shall deem an examination by a surgeon to be appointed by him necessary ; and the fees for each of such examinations, and the requisite certificate thereof, shall be one dollar and fifty cents, which fees shall be paid to the surgeon by the person examined, for which he shall take a receipt, and forward the same to the Pension Office ; and upon the allowance of the claim of the person examined, the Commissioner of Pensions shall furnish to such person an order on the pension agent of his State for the amount of the surgeon's fees.

Sec. 9. *And be it further enacted*, That the Commissioner of Pensions, on application made to him in person or by letter by any claimants or applicants for pension, bounty, or other allowance required by law to

be adjusted and paid by the Pension Office, shall furnish such claimants, free of all expense or charge to them, all such printed instructions
and forms as may be necessary in establishing and obtaining said claim;
and in case such claim is prosecuted by an agent or attorney of such
claimant or applicant, on the issue of a certificate of pension or the
granting of a bounty or allowance, the Commissioner of Pensions shall
forthwith notify the applicant or claimant that such certificate has
been issued or allowance made, and the amount thereof.

SEC. 10. *And be it further enacted*, That the pilots, engineers, sailors,
and crews upon the gunboats and war vessels of the United States,
who have not been regularly mustered into the service of the United
States, shall be entitled to the same bounty allowed to persons of
corresponding rank in the naval service, provided they continue in service to the close of the present war; and all persons serving as aforesaid, who have been or may be wounded or incapacitated for service,
shall be entitled to receive for such disability the pension allowed by
the provisions of this act, to those of like rank, and each and every
such person shall receive pay according to corresponding rank in the
naval service : *Provided*, That no person receiving pension or bounty
under the provisions of this act shall receive either pension or bounty
for any other service in the present war.

SEC. 11 *And be it further enacted*, That the widows and heirs of all
persons described in the last preceding section who have been or may
be employed as aforesaid, or who have been or may be killed in battle,
or of those who have died or shall die of wounds received while so
employed, shall be paid the bounty and pension allowed by the provisions of this act, according to rank, as provided in the last preceding
section.

SEC. 12. *And be it further enacted*, That the Secretary of the Interior
be, and he is hereby, authorized to appoint a special agent for the
Pension Office, to assist in the detection of frauds against the pension
laws, to cause persons committing such frauds to be prosecuted, and
to discharge such other duties as said Secretary may require him to
perform; which said agent shall receive for his services an annual

salary of twelve hundred dollars ; and his actual travelling expenses incurred in the discharge of his duties shall be paid by the government.

SEC. 13. *And be it further enacted*, That all acts and parts of acts inconsistent with the provisions of this act be, and the same are hereby, repealed.

Approved July 14, 1862.

IV..PUBLIC—No. 148.

AN ACT to prevent members of Congress and officers of the Government of the United States from taking consideration for procuring contracts, office, or place from the United States, and for other purposes.

Be it enacted by the Senate and House of Representatives of the United States of America in Congress assembled, That any member of Congress or any officer of the Government of the United States who shall, directly or indirectly, take, receive, or agree to receive, any money, property, or other valuable consideration whatsoever, from any person or persons, for procuring, or aiding to procure, any contract, office, or place from the Government of the United States, or any Department thereof, or from any officer of the United States, for any person or persons whatsoever, or for giving any such contract, office, or place to any person whomsoever, and the person or persons who shall directly or indirectly offer or agree to give, or give, or bestow any money, property, or other valuable consideration whatsoever, for the procuring or aiding to procure any contract, office, or place, as aforesaid, and any member of Congress who shall directly or indirectly take, receive, or agree to receive, any money, property, or other valuable consideration whatsoever after his election as such member, for his attention to, services, action, vote, or decision on any question, matter, cause, or proceeding which may then be pending, or may by law or under the Constitution of the United States be brought before him in his official capacity, or in his place of trust and profit as such member of Congress, shall, for every such offence, be liable to indictment as for a misdemeanor in any court of the United States having jurisdiction thereof, and on conviction thereof shall pay a fine of not exceeding ten thousand dollars, and suffer imprisonment in the penitentiary not exceeding two years, at the discretion of the court trying the same; and any such contract or agreement, as aforesaid, may, at the option of the President of the United States, be declared absolutely null and void; and any member of Congress or officer of the United States convicted, as aforesaid, shall, moreover, be disqualified from holding any office of honor, profit, or trust under the Government of the United States.

Approved July 16, 1862.

V..Public—No. 152.   [Extract.]

Relative rank between Officers of the Army and the Navy.

AN ACT to establish and equalize the grades of line officers of the United States Navy.

○   ○   ○   ○   ○   ○   ○   ○

Sec. 13. *And be it further enacted,* That the relative rank between officers of the navy and the army shall be as follows, lineal rank only to be considered:

Rear admirals with major generals.

Commodores with brigadier generals.

Captains with colonels.

Commanders with lieutenant colonels.

Lieutenant commanders with majors.

Lieutenants with captains.

Masters with first lieutenants.

Ensigns with second lieutenants.

○   ○   ○   ○   ○   ○   ○   ○

Approved July 16, 1862.

VI..Public—No. 159.

AN ACT prohibiting the confinement of persons in the military service of the United States in the penitentiary of the District of Columbia, except as a punishment for certain crimes, and to discharge therefrom certain convicts by sentence of courts-martial, and for other purposes.

Be it enacted by the Senate and House of Representatives of the United States of America in Congress assembled, That hereafter no person in the military service of the United States, convicted and sentenced by a court-martial, shall be punished by confinement in the penitentiary of the District of Columbia, unless the offence of which such person may be convicted would by some statute of the United States or at common law, as the same exists in the said District, subject such convict to said punishment.

SEC. 2. *And be it further enacted,* That all such persons in the military service, as aforesaid, who have heretofore been, or may hereafter be, convicted and sentenced by a court-martial for any offence which, if tried before the criminal court of said District, would not subject such person to imprisonment in said penitentiary, and who are now or may hereafter be confined therein, shall be discharged from said imprisonment, upon such terms and conditions of further punishment as the President of the United States may, in his discretion, impose as a commutation of said sentence.

SEC. 3. *And be it further enacted,* That upon the application of any citizen of the United States, supported by his oath, alleging that a person or persons in the military service, as aforesaid, are confined in said penitentiary under the sentence of a court-martial for any offence not punishable by imprisonment in the penitentiary by the authority of the criminal court aforesaid, it shall be the duty of the judge of said court, or, in case of his absence or inability, of one of the judges of the circuit court of said District, if, upon an inspection of the record of proceedings of said court-martial, he shall find the facts to be as alleged in said application, immediately to issue the writ of habeas corpus to bring before him the said convict; and if, upon an investigation of the case, it shall be the opinion of such judge that the case of such convict is within the provisions of the previous sections of this act, he shall order such convict to be confined in the common jail of said District, until the decision of the President of the United States as to the commutation aforesaid shall be filed in said court, and then such convict shall be disposed of and suffer such punishment as by said commutation of his said sentence may be imposed.

SEC. 4. *And be it further enacted,* That no person convicted upon the decision of a court-martial shall be confined in any penitentiary in the United States, except under the conditions of this act.

Approved July 16, 1862.

VII..By the President of the United States of America:

A Proclamation.

In pursuance of the sixth section of the act of Congress entitled "An act to suppress insurrection, to punish treason and rebellion, to seize and confiscate the property of rebels, and for other purposes," approved July 17, 1862, and which act, and the joint resolution explanatory thereof, are herewith published, I, Abraham Lincoln, President of the United States, do hereby proclaim to and warn all persons within the contemplation of said sixth section to cease participating in, aiding, countenancing, or abetting the existing rebellion, or any rebellion, against the Government of the United States, and to return to their proper allegiance to the United States, on pain of the forfeitures and seizures as within and by said sixth section provided.

In testimony whereof, I have hereunto set my hand and caused the seal of the United States to be affixed.

Done at the city of Washington, this twenty-fifth day of July, in the year of our Lord one thousand eight hundred and sixty-

[L. S.] two, and of the Independence of the United States the eighty-seventh.

ABRAHAM LINCOLN.

By the President:

William H. Seward, *Secretary of State.*

PUBLIC—No. 160.

AN ACT to suppress insurrection, to punish treason and rebellion, to seize and confiscate the property of rebels, and for other purposes.

Be it enacted by the Senate and House of Representatives of the United States of America in Congress assembled, That every person who shall hereafter commit the crime of treason against the United States, and shall be adjudged guilty thereof, shall suffer death, and all his slaves, if any, shall be declared and made free ; or, at the discretion of the court, he shall be imprisoned for not less than five years and fined not less than ten thousand dollars, and all his slaves, if any, shall be declared and made free ; said fine shall be levied and collected on any or all of the property, real and personal, excluding slaves, of which the said person so convicted was the owner at the time of committing the said crime, any sale or conveyance to the contrary notwithstanding.

Sec. 2. *And be it further enacted*, That if any person shall hereafter incite, set on foot, assist, or engage in any rebellion or insurrection against the authority of the United States, or the laws thereof, or shall give aid and comfort thereto, or shall engage in, or give aid and comfort to, any such existing rebellion or insurrection, and be convicted thereof, such person shall be punished by imprisonment for a period not exceeding ten years, or by a fine not exceeding ten thousand dollars, and by the liberation of all his slaves, if any he have ; or by both of said punishments, at the discretion of the court.

Sec. 3. *And be it further enacted*, That every person guilty of either of the offences described in this act shall be forever incapable and disqualified to hold any office under the United States.

Sec. 4. *And be it further enacted*, That this act shall not be construed in any way to affect or alter the prosecution, conviction, or punishment of any person or persons guilty of treason against the United States before the passage of this act, unless such person is convicted under this act.

Sec. 5. *And be it further enacted*, That, to insure the speedy termination of the present rebellion, it shall be the duty of the President of the United States to cause the seizure of all the estate and property, money, stocks, credits, and effects of the persons hereinafter named in this section, and to apply and use the same and the proceeds thereof for the support of the Army of the United States ; that is to say :

First. Of any person hereafter acting as an officer of the army or navy of the rebels in arms against the Government of the United States.

Secondly. Of any person hereafter acting as President, Vice-President, member of Congress, judge of any court, cabinet officer, foreign minister, commissioner or consul of the so-called Confederate States of America.

Thirdly. Of any person acting as Governor of a State, member of a convention or legislature, or judge of any court of any of the so-called Confederate States of America.

Fourthly. Of any person who, having held an office of honor, trust, or profit in the United States, shall hereafter hold an office in the so-called Confederate States of America.

Fifthly. Of any person hereafter holding any office or agency under the government of the so-called Confederate States of America, or under any of the several States of the said Confederacy, or the laws thereof, whether such office or agency be national, state, or municipal in its name or character : *Provided*, That the persons, thirdly, fourthly, and fifthly above described shall have accepted their appointment or election since the date of the pretended ordinance of secession of the State, or shall have taken an oath of allegiance to, or to support the Constitution of, the so-called Confederate States.

Sixthly. Of any person who, owning property in any loyal State or Territory of the United States, or in the District of Columbia, shall hereafter assist and give aid and comfort to such rebellion ; and all sales, transfers, or conveyances of any such property shall be null and void ; and it shall be a sufficient bar to any suit brought by such person for the possession or the use of such property, or any of it, to allege and prove that he is one of the persons described in this section.

SEC. 6. *And be it further enacted*, That if any person within any State or Territory of the United States, other than those named as aforesaid, after the passage of this act, being engaged in armed rebellion against the Government of the United States, or aiding or abetting such rebellion, shall not, within sixty days after public warning and proclamation duly given and made by the President of the United States, cease to aid, countenance, and abet such rebellion, and return to his allegiance to the United States, all the estate and property, moneys, stocks, and credits of such person shall be liable to seizure as aforesaid, and it shall be the duty of the President to seize and use them as aforesaid or the proceeds thereof. And all sales, transfers, or conveyances of any such property after the expiration of the said sixty days from the date of such warning and proclamation shall be null and void ; and it shall be a sufficient bar to any suit brought by such person for the possession or the use of such property, or any of it, to allege and prove that he is one of the persons described in this section.

SEC. 7. *And be it further enacted*, That to secure the condemnation and sale of any such property, after the same shall have been seized, so that it may be made available for the purpose aforesaid, proceedings in rem shall be instituted in the name of the United States in any district court thereof, or in any Territorial court, or in the United States district court for the District of Columbia, within which the property above described, or any part thereof, may be found, or into which the same, if movable, may first be brought, which proceedings shall conform as nearly as may be to proceedings in admiralty or revenue cases; and if said property, whether real or personal, shall be found to have belonged to a person engaged in rebellion, or who has given aid or comfort thereto, the same shall be condemned as enemies' property and become the property of the United States, and may be disposed of as the court shall decree, and the proceeds thereof paid into the Treasury of the United States for the purposes aforesaid.

SEC. 8. *And be it further enacted*, That the several courts aforesaid shall have power to make such orders, establish such forms of decree and sale, and direct such deeds and conveyances to be executed and delivered by the marshals thereof where real estate shall be the subject of sale, as shall fitly and efficiently effect the purposes of this act, and vest in the purchasers of such property good and valid titles thereto. And the said courts shall have power to allow such fees and charges of their officers as shall be reasonable and proper in the premises.

SEC. 9. *And be it further enacted*, That all slaves of persons who shall hereafter be engaged in rebellion against the Government of the United States, or who shall in any way give aid or comfort thereto, escaping from such persons and taking refuge within the lines of the army; and all slaves captured from such persons or deserted by them and coming under the control of the Government of the United States, and all slaves of such persons found *on* [or] being within any place occupied by rebel forces and afterwards occupied by the forces of the United States shall be deemed captives of war, and shall be forever free of their servitude, and not again held as slaves

SEC. 10. *And be it further enacted*, That no slave escaping into any State, Territory, or the District of Columbia, from any other State, shall be delivered up, or in any way impeded or hindered of his liberty, except for crime, or some offence against the laws, unless the person claiming said fugitive shall first make oath that the person to whom the labor or service of such fugitive is alleged to be due is his lawful owner, and has not borne arms against the United States in the present rebellion, nor in any way given aid and comfort thereto; and no person engaged in the military or naval service of the United States shall, under any pretence whatever, assume to decide on the validity of the claim of any person to the service or labor of any other person, or surrender up any such person to the claimant, on pain of being dismissed from the service.

SEC. 11. *And be it further enacted*, That the President of the United States is authorized to employ as many persons of African descent as he may deem necessary and proper for the suppression of this rebellion, and for this purpose he may organize and use them in such manner as he may judge best for the public welfare.

SEC. 12. *And be it further enacted*, That the President of the United States is hereby authorized to make provision for the transportation, colonization, and settlement, in some tropical country beyond the limits of the United States, of such persons of the African race, made free by the provisions of this act, as may be willing to emigrate, having first obtained the consent of the government of said country to their protection and settlement within the same, with all the rights and privileges of freemen.

SEC. 13. *And be it further enacted*, That the President is hereby authorized, at any time hereafter, by proclamation, to extend to persons who may have participated in the existing rebellion in any State or part thereof, pardon and amnesty, with such exceptions and at such time and on such conditions as he may deem expedient for the public welfare.

SEC. 14. *And be it further enacted*, That the courts of the United States shall have full power to institute proceedings, make orders and decrees, issue process, and do all other things necessary to carry this act into effect.

Approved July 17, 1862.

VIII..Public Resolution—No. 54.

JOINT RESOLUTION explanatory of "An act to suppress insurrection, to punish treason and rebellion, to seize and confiscate the property of rebels, and for other purposes."

Resolved by the Senate and House of Representatives of the United States of America in Congress assembled, That the provisions of the third clause of the fifth section of "An act to suppress insurrection, to punish treason and rebellion, to seize and confiscate the property of rebels, and for other purposes," shall be so construed as not to apply to any act or acts done prior to the passage thereof, nor to include any member of a State legislature or judge of any State court who has not, in accepting or entering upon his office, taken an oath to support the constitution of the so-called "Confederate States of America;" nor shall any punishment or proceedings under said act be so construed as to work a forfeiture of the real estate of the offender beyond his natural life.

Approved July 17, 1862.

IX..Public—No. 164.

AN ACT to provide for the more prompt settlement of the accounts of disbursing officers.

Be it enacted by the Senate and House of Representatives of the United States of America in Congress assembled, That from and after the passage of this act any officer or agent of the United States who shall receive public money which he is not authorized to retain as salary, pay, or emolument, shall render his accounts monthly, instead of quarterly, as heretofore ; and such accounts, with the vouchers necessary to the correct and prompt settlement thereof, shall be rendered direct to the proper accounting officer of the Treasury, and be mailed or otherwise forwarded to its proper address within ten days after the expiration of each successive month. And in case of the non-receipt at the Treasury of any accounts within a reasonable and proper time thereafter, the officer whose accounts are in default shall be required to furnish satisfactory evidence of having complied with the provisions of this act ; and for any default on his part the delinquent officer shall be deemed a defaulter, and be subject to all the penalties prescribed by the sixteenth section of the act of August sixth, eighteen hundred and forty-six, " to provide for the better organization of the Treasury, and for the collection, safe-keeping, transfer, and disbursement of the public revenue :" *Provided,* That the Secretary of the Treasury may, if in his opinion the circumstances of the case justify and require it, extend the time hereinbefore prescribed for the rendition of accounts : *And provided, further,* That nothing herein contained shall be construed to restrain the heads of any of the departments from requiring such other returns or reports from the officer or agent subject to the control of such heads of departments as the public interest may require.

Approved July 17, 1862.

X..Public—No. 165.

AN ACT to define the pay and emoluments of certain officers of the army, and for other purposes.

Be it enacted by the Senate and House of Representatives of the United States of America in Congress assembled, That officers of the army entitled to forage for horses shall not be allowed to commute it, but may draw forage in kind for each horse actually kept by them when, and at the place where, they are on duty, not exceeding the number authorized by law : *Provided, however,* That when forage in kind cannot be furnished by the proper department, then, and in all such cases, officers entitled to forage may commute the same according to existing regulations : *And provided, further,* That officers of the army and of volunteers assigned to duty which requires them to be mounted, shall, during the time they are employed on such duty, receive the pay, emoluments, and allowances of cavalry officers of the same grade respectively.

Sec. 2. *And be it further enacted,* That major generals shall be entitled to draw forage in kind for five horses ; brigadier generals for four horses ; colonels, lieutenant colonels, and majors, for two horses each ; captains and lieutenants of cavalry and artillery, or having the cavalry allowance, for two horses each ; and chaplains, for one horse only.

Sec. 3. *And be it further enacted,* That whenever an officer of the army shall employ a soldier as his servant he shall, for each and every month during which said soldier shall be so employed, deduct from his own monthly pay the full amount paid to or expended by the government per month on account of said soldier; and every officer of the army who shall fail to make such deduction shall, on conviction thereof before a general court-martial, be cashiered.

Sec. 4. *And be it further enacted*, That the first section of the act approved August six, eighteen hundred and sixty-one, entitled "An act to increase the pay of privates in the regular army and in the volunteers in the service of the United States, and for other purposes," shall not be so construed, after the passage of this act, as to increase the emoluments of the commissioned officers of the army. And the eighth section of the act of twenty-second July, eighteen hundred and sixty-one, entitled "An act to authorize the employment of volunteers to aid in enforcing the laws and protecting public property," shall be so construed as to give to quartermaster sergeants the same compensation as to regimental commissary sergeants.

Sec. 5. *And be it further enacted*, That so much of the aforesaid act approved twenty-second July, eighteen hundred and sixty-one, as authorizes each regiment of volunteers in the United States service to have twenty-four musicians for a band, and fixes the compensation of the leader of the band, be, and the same is hereby, repealed : and the men composing such bands shall be mustered out of the service within thirty days after the passage of this act.

[The provisions of this section will be forthwith carried into effect. But in mustering the regimental bands out of service, all enlisted men who have been detached from companies to serve in them, but were not originally mustered in as members of the bands, will be returned to duty in their companies. Not having been enlisted as musicians, they are not entitled to discharge as such. With their own consent, *musicians* of regimental bands, instead of being discharged, may be transferred, on their present enlistment, to form the brigade bands authorized by section 6 of this act, at the discretion of the brigade commanders.]

Sec. 6. *And be it further enacted*, That each brigade in the volunteer service may have sixteen musicians as a band, who shall receive the pay and allowances now provided by law for regimental bands, except the leader of the band, who shall receive forty-five dollars per month with the emoluments and allowances of a quartermaster sergeant.

SEC. 7. *And be it further enacted,* That in lieu of the present rate of mileage allowed to officers of the Army when travelling on public duty, where the transportation in kind is not furnished to them by the government, not more than six cents per mile shall hereafter be allowed, unless where an officer is ordered from a station east of the Rocky mountains to one west of the same mountains, or vice versa, when ten cents per mile shall be allowed to him ; and no officer of the Army or Navy of the United States shall be paid mileage except for travel actually performed at his own expense, and in obedience to orders.

SEC. 8. *And be it further enacted,* That so much of section nine of the aforesaid act, approved July twenty-second, eighteen hundred and sixty-one, and of section seven of the "Act providing for the better organization of the military establishment," approved August third, eighteen hundred and sixty-one, as defines the qualifications of chaplains in the Army and volunteers, shall hereafter be construed to read as follows: That no person shall be appointed a chaplain in the United States Army who is not a regularly ordained minister of some religious denomination, and who does not present testimonials of his present good standing as such minister, with a recommendation for his appointment as an Army chaplain from some authorized ecclesiastical body, or not less than five accredited ministers belonging to said religious denomination.

SEC. 9. *And be it further enacted,* That hereafter the compensation of all chaplains in the regular or volunteer service or Army hospitals shall be one hundred dollars per month and two rations a day when on duty; and the chaplains of the permanent hospitals, appointed under the authority of the second section of the act approved May twentieth, eighteen hundred and sixty-two, shall be nominated to the Senate for its advice and consent, and they shall in all respects fill the requirements of the preceding section of this act relative to the appointment of chaplains in the Army and volunteers, and the appointments of

6

chaplains to Army hospitals, heretofore made by the President, are hereby confirmed ; and it is hereby made the duty of each officer commanding a district or post containing hospitals, or a brigade of troops, within thirty days after the reception of the order promulgating this act, to inquire into the fitness, efficiency, and qualifications of the chaplains of hospitals or regiments, and to muster out of service such chaplains as were not appointed in conformity with the requirements of this act, and who have not faithfully discharged the duties of chaplains during the time they have been engaged as such. Chaplains employed at the military posts called "chaplain posts" shall be required to reside at the posts, and all chaplains in the United States service shall be subject to such rules in relation to leave of absence from duty as are prescribed for commissioned officers of the United States Army stationed at such posts.

Sec. 10. *And be it further enacted*, That so much of the fifth section of the act approved July twenty-second, eighteen hundred and sixty-one, as allows forty cents per day for the use and risk of the horses of company officers of cavalry, and the tenth section of the aforesaid act, approved August three, eighteen hundred and sixty-one, be, and the same are hereby, repealed.

Sec. 11. *And be it further enacted*, That whenever an officer shall be put under arrest, except at remote military posts or stations, it shall be the duty of the officer by whose orders he is arrested to see that a copy of the charges on which he has been arrested and is to be tried shall be served upon him within eight days thereafter, and that he shall be brought to trial within ten days thereafter, unless the necessities of the service prevent such trial ; and then he shall be brought to trial within thirty days after the expiration of the said ten days or the arrest shall cease : *Provided*, That if the copy of the charges be not served upon the arrested officer, as herein provided, the arrest shall cease ; but officers released from arrest under the provisions of this section may be tried whenever the exigencies of the service will permit, within twelve months after such release from arrest : *And provided, further*, That the provisions of this section shall apply to all persons now under arrest and awaiting trial.

o   o   o   o   o   o   o   o

Sec. 13. *And be it further enacted,* That all contracts made for, or orders given for the purchase of, goods or supplies by any department of the government shall be promptly reported to Congress by the proper head of such department if Congress shall at the time be in session, and if not in session said reports shall be made at the commencement of the next ensuing session.

Sec. 14. *And be it further enacted,* That no contract or order, or any interest therein, shall be transferred by the party or parties to whom such contract or order may be given, to any other party or parties, and that any such transfer shall cause the annulment of the contract or order transferred, so far as the United States are concerned : *Provided,* That all rights of action are hereby reserved to the United States for any breach of such contract by the contracting party or parties.

Sec. 15. *And be it further enacted,* That every person who shall furnish supplies of any kind to the army or navy shall be required to mark and distinguish the same, with the name or names of the contractors so furnishing said supplies, in such manner as the Secretary of War and the Secretary of the Navy may respectively direct, and no supplies of any kind shall be received unless so marked and distinguished.

Sec. 16. *And be it further enacted,* That whenever any contractor for subsistence, clothing, arms, ammunition, munitions of war, and for every description of supplies for the army or navy of the United States, shall be found guilty by a court-martial of fraud or wilful neglect of duty, he shall be punished by fine, imprisonment, or such other punishment as the court-martial shall adjudge; and any person who shall contract to furnish supplies of any kind or description for the army or navy, he shall be deemed and taken as a part of the land or naval forces of the United States for which he shall contract to furnish said supplies, and be subject to the rules and regulations for the government of the land and naval forces of the United States.

Sec. 17. *And be it further enacted,* That the President of the United States be, and hereby is, authorized and requested to dismiss and discharge from the military service, either in the army, navy, marine corps, or volunteer force, in the United States service, any officer for any cause which, in his judgment, either renders such officer unsuitable for, or whose dismission would promote, the public service.

Sec. 18. *And be it further enacted,* That the President of the United States shall have power, whenever in his opinion it shall be expedient, to purchase cemetery grounds, and cause them to be securely enclosed, to be used as a national cemetery for the soldiers who shall die in the service of the country.

Sec. 19. *And be it further enacted,* That so much of the act approved the fifth of August, eighteen hundred and sixty-one, entitled "An act supplementary to an act entitled 'An act to increase the present military establishment of the United States,'" approved the twenty-ninth of July, eighteen hundred and sixty-one, as authorizes the appointment of additional aides-de-camp, be, and the same is hereby, repealed. But this repeal shall not be construed so as to deprive those persons already appointed, in strict conformity with said act of the fifth of August, eighteen hundred and sixty-one, from holding their offices in the same manner as if it had not been repealed.

Sec. 20. *And be it further enacted,* That the different regiments and independent companies heretofore mustered into the service of the United States as volunteer engineers, pioneers, or sappers and miners, under the orders of the President or Secretary of War, or by authority of the commanding general of any military department of the United States, or which, having been mustered into the service as infantry, shall have been reorganized and employed as engineers, pioneers, or sappers and miners, shall be, and the same are hereby, recognized and accepted as volunteer engineers, on the same footing, in all respects, in regard to their organization, pay, and emoluments, as the corps of engineers of the regular army of the United States, and they shall be paid for their services, already performed, as is now provided by law for the payment of officers, non-commissioned officers, and privates of the engineer corps of the regular army.

Sec. 21. *And be it further enacted,* That any alien of the age of twenty-one years and upwards, who has enlisted or shall enlist in the armies of the United States, either the regular or the volunteer forces, and has been or shall be hereafter honorably discharged, may be admitted to become a citizen of the United States, upon his petition, without any previous declaration of his intention to become a citizen of the United States, and that he shall not be required to prove more than one year's residence within the United States previous to his application to become such citizen ; and that the court admitting such alien shall, in addition to such proof of residence and good moral character as is now provided by law, be satisfied by competent proof of such person having been honorably discharged from the service of the United States as aforesaid.

○　　　　○　　　　○　　　　○　　　　○

Approved July 17, 1862.

XI..Public—No. 166.

AN ACT to amend the act calling forth the militia to execute the laws of the Union, suppress insurrections, and repel invasions, approved February twenty-eight, seventeen hundred and ninety-five, and the acts amendatory thereof, and for other purposes.

Be it enacted by the Senate and House of Representatives of the United States of America in Congress assembled, That whenever the President of the United States shall call forth the militia of the States, to be employed in the service of the United States, he may specify in his call the period for which such service will be required, not exceeding nine months ; and the militia so called shall be mustered in and continue to serve for and during the term so specified, unless sooner discharged by command of the President. If, by reason of defects in existing laws, or in the execution of them, in the several States, or any of them, it shall be found necessary to provide for enrolling the militia and otherwise putting this act into execution, the President is authorized in such cases to make all necessary rules and regulations ; and the enrolment of the militia shall in all cases include all able-bodied male citizens between the ages of eighteen and forty-five, and shall be apportioned among the States according to representative population.

Sec. 2. *And be it further enacted,* That the militia, when so called into service, shall be organized in the mode prescribed by law for volunteers.

Sec. 3. *And be it further enacted,* That the President be, and he is hereby, authorized, in addition to the volunteer forces which he is now authorized by law to raise, to accept the services of any number of volunteers, not exceeding one hundred thousand, as infantry, for a period of nine months, unless sooner discharged. And every soldier who shall enlist under the provisions of this section shall receive his first month's pay, and also twenty-five dollars as bounty, upon the mustering of his company or regiment into the service of the United States. And all provisions of law relating to volunteers enlisted in the service of the United States for three years, or during the war, except in relation to bounty, shall be, and the same are, extended to, and are hereby declared to embrace, the volunteers to be raised under the provisions of this section.

SEC. 4. *And be it further enacted*, That, for the purpose of filling up the regiments of infantry now in the United States service, the President be, and he hereby is, authorized to accept the services of volunteers in such numbers as may be presented for that purpose, for twelve months, if not sooner discharged. And such volunteers, when mustered into the service, shall be in all respects upon a footing with similar troops in the United States service, except as to service bounty, which shall be fifty dollars, one half of which to be paid upon their joining their regiments, and the other half at the expiration of their enlistment.

SEC. 5. *And be it further enacted*, That the President shall appoint, by and with the advice and consent of the Senate, a judge advocate general, with the rank, pay, and emoluments of a colonel of cavalry, to whose office shall be returned for revision the records and proceedings of all courts-martial and military commissions, and where a record shall be kept of all proceedings had thereupon. And no sentence of death or imprisonment in the penitentiary shall be carried into execution until the same shall have been approved by the President.

SEC. 6 *And be it further enacted*, That there may be appointed by the President, by and with the advice and consent of the Senate, for each army in the field, a judge advocate, with the rank, pay, and emoluments, each, of a major of cavalry, who shall perform the duties of judge advocate for the army to which they respectively belong, under the direction of the judge advocate general.

Sec 7. *And be it further enacted,* That hereafter all offenders in the army charged with offences now punishable by a regimental or garrison court-martial shall be brought before a field officer of his regiment, who shall be detailed for that purpose, and who shall hear and determine the offence, and order the punishment that shall be inflicted; and shall also make a record of his proceedings, and submit the same to the brigade commander, who, upon the approval of the proceedings of such field officer, shall order the same to be executed: *Provided,* That the punishment in such cases be limited to that authorized to be inflicted by a regimental or garrison court-martial. *And provided, further,* That, in the event of there being no brigade commander, the proceedings as aforesaid shall be submitted for approval to the commanding officer of the post.

Sec 8. *And be it further enacted,* That all officers who have been mustered into the service of the United States as battalion adjuncts and quartermasters of cavalry under the orders of the War Department, exceeding the number authorized by law, shall be paid as such for the time they were actually employed in the service of the United States, and that all such officers now in service, exceeding the number as aforesaid, shall be immediately mustered out of the service of the United States.

Sec 9. *And be it further enacted,* That the President be, and he is hereby, authorized to establish and organize army corps according to his discretion.

Sec. 10. *And be it further enacted,* That each army corps shall have the following officers, and no more, attached thereto, who shall constitute the staff of the commander thereof: one assistant adjutant general, one quartermaster, one commissary of subsistence, and one assistant inspector general, who shall bear, respectively, the rank of lieutenant colonel, and who shall be assigned from the army or volunteer force by the President. Also three aides-de-camp, one to bear the rank of major, and two to bear the rank of captain, to be appointed by the President, by and with the advice and consent of the Senate, upon the recommendation of the commander of the army corps. The senior officer of artillery in each army corps shall, in addition to his other duties, act as chief of artillery and ordnance at the headquarters o the corps.

88

SEC. 11. *And be it further enacted,* That the cavalry forces in the service of the United States shall hereafter be organized as follows: Each regiment of cavalry shall have one colonel, one lieutenant colonel, three majors, one surgeon, one assistant surgeon, one regimental adjutant, one regimental quartermaster, one regimental commissary, one sergeant major, one quartermaster sergeant, one commissary sergeant, two hospital stewards, one saddler sergeant, one chief trumpeter, and one chief farrier or blacksmith, and each regiment shall consist of twelve companies or troops, and each company or troop shall have one captain, one first lieutenant, one second lieutenant, and one supernumerary second lieutenant, one first sergeant, one quartermaster sergeant, one commissary sergeant, five sergeants, eight corporals, two teamsters, two farriers or blacksmiths, one saddler, one wagoner, and seventy-eight privates; the regimental adjutants, the regimental quartermasters, and regimental commissaries to be taken from their respective regiments: *Provided,* That vacancies caused by this organization shall not be considered as original, but shall be filled by regular promotion.

SEC. 12. *And be it further enacted,* That the President be, and he is hereby, authorized to receive into the service of the United States, for the purpose of constructing intrenchments, or performing camp service, or any other labor or any military or naval service for which they may be found competent, persons of African descent, and such persons shall be enrolled and organized under such regulations, not inconsistent with the Constitution and laws, as the President may prescribe.

SEC. 13. *And be it further enacted,* That when any man or boy of African descent, who by the laws of any State shall owe service or labor to any person who, during the present rebellion, has levied war or has borne arms against the United States, or adhered to their enemies by giving them aid and comfort, shall render any such servive as is provided for in this act, he, his mother, and his wife and children, shall forever thereafter be free, any law, usage, or custom whatsoever to the contrary notwithstanding: *Provided,* That the mother, wife, and children of such man or boy of African descent shall not be made free by the operation of this act, except where such mother, wife, or children owe service or labor to some person who during the present rebellion, has borne arms against the United States, or adhered to their enemies by giving them aid and comfort.

SEC. 14. *And be it further enacted*, That the expenses incurred to carry this act into effect shall be paid out of the general appropriation for the army and volunteers.

SEC. 15. *And be it further enacted*, That all persons who have been or shall be hereafter enrolled in the service of the United States under this act shall receive the pay and rations now allowed by law to soldiers, according to their respective grades: *Provided*, That persons of African descent, who under this law shall be employed, shall receive ten dollars per month and one ration, three dollars of which monthly pay may be in clothing.

SEC. 16. *And be it further enacted*, That medical purveyors and store-keepers shall give bonds in such sums as the Secretary of War may require, with security to be approved by him.

Approved July 17, 1862.

o   o   o   o   o   o   o

XIV..PUBLIC—No. 168.

AN ACT to suspend temporarily the operation of an act entitled "An act to prevent and punish fraud on the part of officers intrusted with making of contracts for the Government," approved June two, eighteen hundred and sixty-two.—[*See Gen. Orders, No.* 58.]

Be it enacted by the Senate and House of Representatives of the United States of America in Congress assembled, That the operation of the act entitled "An act to prevent and punish frauds on the part of officers intrusted with making of contracts for the Government," approved June two, eighteen hundred and sixty-two, be and the same is hereby suspended until the first Monday of January, eighteen hundred and sixty-three.

Approved July 17, 1862.

BY ORDER OF THE SECRETARY OF WAR:

E. D. TOWNSEND,
Assistant Adjutant General.

GENERAL ORDERS, } WAR DEPARTMENT,
 ADJUTANT GENERAL'S OFFICE,
No. 92. } *Washington, July* 31, 1862.

The following Order is published for the information of all concerned:

WAR DEPARTMENT,

Washington Ci'y, D. C., July 31, 1862.

. The absence of officers and privates from their duty under various pretexts, while receiving pay, at great expense and burden to the Government, makes it necessary that efficient measures be taken to enforce their return to duty, or that their places be supplied by those who will not take pay while rendering no service. This evil, moreover, tends greatly to discourage the patriotic impulses of those who would contribute to support the families of faithful soldiers.

It is therefore ordered by the President—

I..That on Monday, the 11th day of August, all leaves of absence and furloughs by whomsoever given, unless by the War Department, are revoked and absolutely annulled, and all officers capable of service are required forthwith to join their respective commands, and all privates capable of service to join their regiments, under penalty of dismissal from the service, or such penalty as a Court-Martial may award, unless the absence be occasioned by lawful cause.

II..The only excuses allowed for the absence of officers or privates after the 11th day of August are :

1st. The order or leave of the War Department.

2d. Disability from wounds received in service.

3d. Disability from disease that renders the party unfit for military duty. But any officer or private whose health permits him to visit watering places or places of amusement, or to make social visits, or walk about the town, city, or neighborhood in which he may be, will ` isidered fit for military duty, and as evading duty by absence from his command or ranks.

III..On Monday, the eighteenth day of August, at 10 o'clock a. m., each Regiment and Corps shall be mustered. The absentees will be marked, three lists of the same made out, and, within forty-eight hours after the muster, one copy shall be sent to the Adjutant General of the Army, one to the Commander of the Corps, the third to be retained ; and all officers and privates fit for duty absent at that time will be regarded as absent without cause, their pay will be stopped, and they dismissed from the service, or treated as deserters, unless restored ; and no officer shall be restored to his rank unless by the judgment of a Court of Inquiry, to be approved by the President, he shall establish that his absence was with good cause.

IV...Commanders of Corps, Divisions, Brigades, Regiments, and detached Posts, are strictly enjoined to enforce the muster and return aforesaid. Any officer failing in his duty herein will be deemed guilty of gross neglect of duty, and be dismissed from the service.

V...A commissioner shall be appointed by the Secretary of War to superintend the execution of this order in the respective States.

The United States marshals in the respective districts, the mayor and chief of police of any town or city, the sheriff of the respective counties in each State, all postmasters and justices of the peace, are authorized to act as special provost marshals to arrest any officer or private soldier, fit for duty, who may be found absent from his command without just cause, and convey him to the nearest military post or depot. The transportation, reasonable expenses of this duty, and five dollars, will be paid for each officer or private so arrested and delivered.

By Order of the President :

E. M. STANTON,
Secretary of War.

By Order of the Secretary of War :

E. D. TOWNSEND,
Assistant Adjutant General.

GENERAL ORDERS, }   WAR DEPARTMENT,
                ADJUTANT GENERAL'S OFFICE,
No. 94. }   *Washington, August* 4, 1862.

The following order is published for the information of all concerned :

WAR DEPARTMENT,
Washington City, D. C., August 4, 1862.

Ordered :

I...That a draft of three hundred thousand militia be immediately called into the service of the United States, to serve for nine months unless sooner discharged. The Secretary of War will assign the quotas to the States, and establish regulations for the draft.

II..That if any State shall not, by the fifteenth of August, furnish its quota of the additional three hundred thousand volunteers authorized by law, the deficiency of volunteers in that State will also be made up by special draft from the militia. The Secretary of War will establish regulations for this purpose.

III..Regulations will be prepared by the War Department, and presented to the President, with the object of securing the promotion of officers of the Army and Volunteers for meritorious and distinguished services, and of preventing the nomination or appointment in the military service of incompetent or unworthy officers. The regulations will also provide for ridding the service of such incompetent persons as now hold commissions in it.

BY ORDER OF THE PRESIDENT:

EDWIN M. STANTON,
Secretary of War.

BY ORDER OF THE SECRETARY OF WAR:

E. D. TOWNSEND,
Assistant Adjutant General.

GENERAL ORDERS, }   WAR DEPARTMENT,
                      ADJUTANT GENERAL'S OFFICE,
No. 95. }   *Washington, August 5*, 1862.

The following orders are promulgated for the information of all concerned:

WAR DEPARTMENT,
Washington City, D. C., July 31, 1862.

I..*Ordered*, That the Hon. L. C. TURNER, of New York, be, and he is hereby, appointed Associate Judge Advocate for the Army around Washington. That all cases of State prisoners, and also cases of military arrests in the District of Columbia and the adjacent counties of Virginia, are specially assigned to him for investigation and determination. The Military Governor of the District of Columbia, and the

Provost Marshal of Washington, will make report to him of cases wherein the action of a Judge Advccate may be required.

II.._Ordered_, That SIMEON DRAPER, Esquire, of New York, be, and he is hereby, appointed a Commissioner of this Department, to superintend the execution of the order of this date [General Orders, No. 92] respecting absentee officers and privates. He will have an office assigned to him in the War Department, and will communicate with the Marshals, Mayors, Chiefs of Police, and other special Provost Marshals designated in said order. All communications touching the execution of said order will be addressed to him. Quartermasters and Commissaries will furnish transportation and subsistence on his requisition, and all officers in the service will aid him in the duties of his commission.

EDWIN M. STANTON,
Secretary of War.

BY ORDER OF THE SECRETARY OF WAR:

E. D. TOWNSEND,
Assistant Adjutant General.

GENERAL ORDERS,	WAR DEPARTMENT,
	ADJUTANT GENERAL'S OFFICE,
No. 97.	_Washington, August_ 7, 1862.

I.._Commanders of Volunteer Regiments are reminded that the clothing accounts of their men must be settled after they have been one year in service, and the balance stated on the first subsequent muster roll. Where this has not already been done at the June muster, the omission must be supplied on the next rolls for pay, or they cannot be recognized as valid.

II.._Parcels directed to the Adjutant General of the Army will hereafter be marked on the right-hand upper corner in a way to indicate their contents. Those pertaining to the _Volunteer_ Recruiting Service will be so marked, to distinguish them from those relating to the Regular Service, which are examined in a different office. Packages containing certificates of disability, Regular and Volunteer muster rolls, returns, &c., will all be marked in like manner.

III..The attention of Sutlers, and all others concerned, is directed to the second section of the act of March 3, 1855, which provides that it shall not be lawful for any postmaster or other person to sell any postage stamp or stamped envelope for any larger sum than that indicated upon the face of such postage stamp, or for any larger sum than that charged therefor by the Post Office Department ; and that any person who shall violate this provision shall be deemed guilty of a misdemeanor, and, on conviction thereof, shall be fined in any sum not less than ten nor more than five hundred dollars.

BY ORDER OF THE SECRETARY OF WAR :

E. D. TOWNSEND,

Assistant Adjutant General.

GENERAL ORDERS, | WAR DEPARTMENT,
No. 99. | ADJUTANT GENERAL'S OFFICE,
| *Washington, August* 9, 1862.

REGULATIONS FOR THE ENROLMENT AND DRAFT OF THREE HUNDRED THOUSAND MILITIA.

In pursuance of an Order by the President of the United States, bearing date August 4, 1862, whereby it is provided that a draft of three hundred thousand militia be immediately called into the service of the United States to serve for nine months, unless sooner discharged, and that the Secretary of War shall assign the quotas to the States and establish regulations for the draft ; also, that if any State shall not by the 15th of August furnish its quota of the additional three hundred thousand volunteers authorized by law, the deficiency of volunteers in that State shall also be made up by special draft from the militia, and that the Secretary of War shall establish regulations for this purpose —
IT IS ORDERED :

First. The Governors of the respective States will proceed forthwith to furnish their respective quotas of three hundred thousand militia called for by the Order of the President, dated the fourth day of August. 1862, which quotas have been furnished to the Governors respectively by communication from this Department of this date according to the regulations hereinafter set forth.

Second. The Governors of the several States are hereby requested forthwith to designate rendezvous for the drafted militia of said States, and to appoint commandants therefor, and to notify the Secretary of War of the location of such rendezvous and the names of the commandants.

It is important that the rendezvous should be few in number, and located with a view to convenience of transportation.

Third. The Governors of the respective States will cause an enrolment to be made forthwith by the assessors of the several counties, or by any other officers to be appointed by such Governors, of all ablebodied male citizens, between the ages of eighteen and forty-five, within the respective counties, giving the name, age, and occupation of each, together with remarks showing whether he is in the service of the United States, and in what capacity, and any other facts which may determine his exemption from military duty.

All reasonable and proper expenses of such enrolment, and of the draft hereinafter provided, will be reimbursed by the United States upon vouchers showing the detailed statement of service performed and expenses incurred, to be approved by such Governors.

Fourth. Where no provision is made by law in any State for carrying into effect the draft hereby ordered, or where such provisions are in any manner defective, such draft shall be conducted as follows :

1. Immediately upon completion of the enrolment, the lists of enrolled persons shall be filed in the offices of the sheriffs of the counties in which such enrolled persons reside.

2. The governors of the several States shall appoint a commissioner for each county of their respective States, whose duty it shall be to superintend the drafting, and hear and determine the excuses of persons claiming to be exempt from military duty. Such commissioner shall receive a compensation of four dollars per diem for each day he may be actually employed in the discharge of his duties as such commissioner.

3. The enrolling officer shall immediately, upon the filing of the enrolment lists, notify said commissioner that said lists have been so filed, and the commissioner shall thereupon give notice, by handbills

posted in each township of his county, of the time and place at which claims of exemption will be received and determined by him, and shall fix the time to be specified in the order aforesaid within ten days of the filing of the enrolment at which the draft shall be made, and all persons claiming to be exempt from military duty shall, before the day fixed for the draft, make proof of such exemption before said commissioner, and if found sufficient, his name shall be stricken from the list by a line drawn through it, leaving it still legible.

The commissioner shall, in like manner, strike from the list the names of all persons now in the military service of the United States; all telegraph operators and constructors actually engaged on the fifth day of August, 1862; all engineers of locomotives on railroads; all artificers and workmen employed in any public arsenal or armory; the Vice President of the United States; the officers, judicial and executive, of the government of the United States; the members of both houses of Congress and their respective officers; all custom-house officers and their clerks; all post officers and stage drivers who are employed in the care and conveyance of the mail of the post office of the United States; all ferrymen who are employed at any ferry on the post road; all pilots; all mariners actually employed in the sea service of any citizen or merchant within the United States; all engineers and pilots of registered or licensed steamboats and steamships; and all persons exempted by the laws of the respective States from military duty, on sufficient evidence, or on his personal knowledge that said persons belong to any of the aforesaid classes, whether the exemption is claimed by them or not.

Exemption will not be made for disability, unless it be of such permanent character as to render the person unfit for service for a period of more than thirty days, to be certified by a surgeon appointed by the governor, in each county, for that purpose.

5. At the time fixed, as before provided by the commissioner, for making the draft, the sheriff of the county, or, in his absence, such person as the commissioner may appoint, shall, in the presence of said commissioner, publicly place in a wheel or box, of a like character to such as are used for drawing jurors, separate folded ballots, containing

the names of all persons remaining on said enrolment lists not stricken off as before provided, and a proper person, appointed by the com missioner, and blindfolded, shall thereupon draw from said box or wheel a number of ballots, equal to the number of drafted men fixed by the governor of such State as the proper quota of such county.

6. A printed or written notice of his enrolment and draft, and of the place of rendezvous of the drafted military force, shall thereupon be served by a person to be appointed by the commissioner, upon each person so drafted, either by delivering the same in person or by leaving it at his last known place of residence.

7. Any person so drafted may offer a substitute at the time of the rendezvous of the drafted militia force, and such substitute, if he shall be an able-bodied man, between the ages of eighteen and forty-five years, and shall consent in writing (with the consent of his parent or guardian, if a minor) to subject himself to all the duties and obligations to which his principal would have been subject, had he personally served, shall be accepted in lieu of such principal.

8. The persons thus drafted shall assemble at the county seat of their respective counties, within five days after the time of drafting, whence transportation will be furnished them by the Governors of the several States to the place of rendezvous.

9. As soon as the draft has been made and the names marked on the enrolment lists, the commissioner will send a copy of the draft to the commandant of rendezvous, and another of the same to the Adjutant General of the State, who will immediately organize the drafted men into companies and regiments of infantry, by assigning one hundred and one men to each company, and ten companies to each regiment, and send a copy of the organization to the commandant of the rendezvous.

10. At the expiration of the time allowed for the drafted men to reach the rendezvous, the commandant shall proceed to complete the organization of the companies and regiments by proclaiming the names of the regimental commissioned officers, which shall be designated in accordance with the laws of the respective States, the number and grade being the same as in the volunteer service; and in case the laws

7

of any State shall provide for the election of officers, they shall be elected under the direction of the commandant of the rendezvous, and reported forthwith to the Governors of such States in order that they may be commissioned, and the non-commissioned officers may be appointed either before or after muster, as the colonel of the regiment shall decide.

11. As soon as the officers of the companies and regiments are designated, the muster-rolls shall be made out under the direction of the commandant of the rendezvous, and the troops inspected and mustered into the service of the United States by the mustering officer appointed for that purpose.

12. In States where enlistments have been made by municipalities and towns, instead of counties, the Governors of such States are authorized to apply the foregoing rules of draft to such municipalities and towns, instead of counties.

Fifth. Provost Marshals will be appointed by the War Department in the Several States, on the nomination of the Governor thereof, with such assistants as may be necessary to enforce the attendance of all drafted persons who shall fail to attend at such places of rendezvous.

Sixth. In case any State shall not, by the 15th day of August, furnish its quota of the additional three hundred thousand volunteers called for by the President on the 2d day of July, 1862, unless otherwise ordered, all incomplete regiments shall then be consolidated, under the direction of the Governors of the respective States, and an additional draft shall be made, as before provided, sufficient to fill up such quota; the number to be drafted from each county of the State to be fixed by the Governor thereof.

Seventh. From and after the 15th day of August, no new regiments of Volunteers will be organized, but the premium, bounty, and advance pay will continue to be paid to those volunteering to go into the old Regiments.

AFTER ORDER, AUGUST 14, 1862.

Eighth. That in filling all requisitions for militia, the quotas of the several States will be apportioned by the Governors among the several counties and (where practicable) among the subdivisions of counties, so that allowance shall be made to such counties and subdivisions for all volunteers theretofore furnished by them and mustered into the service of the *United States*, and whose stipulated term of service shall not have expired.

BY ORDER OF THE SECRETARY OF WAR:

L. THOMAS,
Adjutant General.

GENERAL ORDERS, }   WAR DEPARTMENT,
                   ADJUTANT GENERAL'S OFFICE,

No. 100. }   *Washington, August 11, 1862*

I..So much of General Orders, No. 61, current series, as relates to the *extension* of sick leaves of absence is hereby revoked, and no applications for such extensions need hereafter be made. The order of the President dated July 31, [General Orders, No. 92,] fully explains what may be considered as good cause for absence. Surgeon's certificates of disability, required by existing orders and regulations, must be forwarded not only to the Adjutant General of the Army, but also to the Commander of the Regiment, or, in case of a staff officer, to his Commanding General.

II..Officers absent from duty without leave, or beyond the time of their leaves, will not be allowed to draw pay until a court or commission, which will be ordered on their return to their post or command, shall determine whether there was sufficient cause for their absence. They will accordingly provide themselves with a full description of the nature and cause of their disability, certified by the proper medical authority, as required by existing orders and regulations.

III..Officers of volunteers who are absent from duty on account of disease contracted before they entered service, will be immediately mustered out. Those who have been absent for more than sixty days on account of wounds or disease contracted in the line of their duty, and who are still unable to return to duty, will be reported to the Adjutant General of the Army for discharge, in order that their places may be filled by others fit for field service. For this class of officers Congress has provided pensions.

IV..Applications for pensions must be made to the Commissioner of Pensions, who is the Judge of the sufficiency of evidence in support of such claims, and who furnishes the forms and regulations relating thereto.

V..When an officer returns to his command after having overstaid his leave of absence, he may be tried by a court-martial for this as a military offence, or a commission may be appointed by the commanding officer of his division, army corps, or army, as the case may be, to investigate his case, and to determine whether or not he was absent from proper cause ; and if there should be found to be such proper cause, he will be entitled to pay during such absence. The proceedings of such commission will be sent to the Adjutant General of the Army for the approval of the Secretary of War. Such commissions will consist of not less than three nor over five commissioned officers.

VI..Where troops are serving in an army corps, or an army, no leaves of absence will be granted on the certificate of a regimental or brigade surgeon till the same has been approved by the medical director of such army corps or army ; and no medical director will indorse any certificate until he has made a personal examination of the applicant, or received a favorable report from a medical officer appointed by him to make such personal examination. And if upon such personal examination it be found that the certificate of disability was given without proper cause, the name of the medical officer giving it will be reported to the Adjutant General of the Army, in order that he may be dismissed from the service.

VII..Where officers are not serving in a division, army corps, or separate army, applications for leaves may be made to the Adjutant General of the Army ; but, except in very extraordinary cases, no leave of absence will be granted unless the application be accompanied by a certificate of the same character as that prescribed in General Orders, No. 61.

VIII..In all cases of personal application for leaves of absence made to the War Department, the applicant will be examined by a medical officer assigned to that duty in this city.

BY ORDER OF THE SECRETARY OF WAR:

E. D. TOWNSEND,
Assistant Adjutant General.

GENERAL ORDERS, }   WAR DEPARTMENT,
ADJUTANT GENERAL'S OFFICE,
No. 102. }   *Washington, August* 11, 1862.

All leaves of absence and furloughs, by whomsoever given, unless by the War Department, are, from this date, null and void, and all officers and privates capable of service will immediately rejoin their respective commands. The commanding officer of each corps, regiment, military post, or other command, will see that the muster directed in General Orders, No. 92, current series, be made on the 18th instant, and that all absentees be marked as therein directed. All persons so marked as absent will be considered as absent without proper cause until they shall adduce evidence before a military court or commission to show that such absence was occasioned by one of the three causes specified in General Orders, No 92; and until the action of such court or commission they will receive no pay.

BY COMMAND OF MAJOR GENERAL HALLECK:

E. D. TOWNSEND,
Assistant Adjutant General.

GENERAL ORDERS, }   WAR DEPARTMENT,
ADJUTANT GENERAL'S OFFICE,
No. 104. }   *Washington, August* 13, 1862.

The following orders are published for the information and guidance of all concerned:

I..   WAR DEPARTMENT,
Washington City, D. C., August 8, 1862.

By direction of the President of the United States, it is hereby ordered that, until further order, no citizen liable to be drafted into the militia shall be allowed to go to a foreign country. And all marshals, deputy marshals, and military officers of the United States are directed, and all police authorities, especially at the ports of the United States on the seaboard and on the frontier, are requested, to see that this order is faithfully carried into effect. And they are hereby authorized and directed to arrest and detain any person or persons about to depart from the United States in violation of this order, and report to Major L. C. Turner, Judge Advocate, at Washington City, for further instructions respecting the person or persons so arrested or detained.

2. Any person liable to draft who shall absent himself from his county or State before such draft is made will be arrested by any provost marshal or other United States or State officer wherever he may be found within the jurisdiction of the United States, and be conveyed to the nearest military post or depot and placed on military duty for the term of the draft; and the expenses of his own arrest and conveyance to such post or depot, and also the sum of five dollars as a reward to the officer who shall make such arrest, shall be deducted from his pay.

3. The writ of habeas corpus is hereby suspended in respect to all persons so arrested and detained, and in respect to all persons arrested for disloyal practices.

EDWIN M. STANTON,
Secretary of War.

II.__   WAR DEPARTMENT,
Washington City, D. C., August 11, 1862.

The temporary restrictions upon travelling, deemed necessary to prevent evasions of liability to be drafted into the militia, were not intended to apply to couriers with despatches to and from the legations of friendly powers in the United States. All authorities, civil and military, are consequently required to allow such couriers to pass freely, without let or molestation.

EDWIN M. STANTON,
Secretary of War.

BY ORDER OF THE SECRETARY OF WAR:

E. D. TOWNSEND,
Assistant Adjutant General.

GENERAL ORDERS,   WAR DEPARTMENT,
                      ADJUTANT GENERAL'S OFFICE,

No. 105.   *Washington, August* 14, 1862.

The inspection of all cavalry forces, preparatory to their being mustered into the service of the United States, shall hereafter comprise, in addition to the usual personal examination, a test of horsemanship, to be made under the direction of the mustering officer; and no person shall be mustered into the cavalry service who does not exhibit good horsemanship and a practical knowledge of the ordinary care and treatment of horses.

BY ORDER OF THE SECRETARY OF WAR:

E. D. TOWNSEND,
Assistant Adjutant General.

GENERAL ORDERS,   WAR DEPARTMENT,
                      ADJUTANT GENERAL'S OFFICE,

No. 107.   *Washington, August* 15, 1862.

I..Officers of the regular army will, as a general rule, receive leaves of absence to accept the rank of Colonel in volunteer regiments, but not lower grades. Non-commissioned officers and privates will be discharged on receiving commissions in volunteer regiments.

II..The oath of allegiance will not be administered to any person against his own will; it must in all cases be a voluntary act on his part. Nor will any compulsory parole of honor be received. But oaths taken, and paroles given, to avoid arrest, detention, imprisonment, or expulsion, are voluntary or free acts, and cannot be regarded as compulsory. All persons guilty of violating such oaths or paroles will be punished according to the laws and usages of war.

III..The laws of the United States and the general laws of war, authorize, in certain cases, the seizure and conversion of private property for the subsistence, transportation, and other uses of the army; but this must be distinguished from pillage, and the taking of property for *public* purposes is very different from its conversion to *private* uses. All property lawfully taken from the enemy, or from the inhabit-ants of an enemy's country, instantly becomes *public* property, and must be used and accounted for as such. The 52d Article of War authorizes the penalty of death for pillage or plundering, and other articles authorize severe punishments for any officer or soldier who shall sell, embezzle, misapply, or waste military stores, or who shall permit the waste or misapplication of any such public property. The penalty is the same whether the offence be committed in our own or in an enemy's territory.

IV..All property, public or private, taken from alleged enemies, must be inventoried and duly accounted for. If the property taken be claimed as private, receipts must be given to such claimants or their agents. Officers will be held strictly accountable for all property taken by them or by their authority, and it must be returned for, the same as any other public property.

V..Where foraging parties are sent out for provisions or other stores, the commanding officer of such party will be held accountable for the conduct of his command, and will make a true report of all property taken.

VI..No officer or soldier will, without authority, leave his colors or ranks, to take private property, or to enter a private house for that purpose. All such acts are punishable with death, and an officer who permits them is equally as guilty as the actual pillager.

VII..Commanding officers of armies and corps will be held responsible for the execution of these orders in their respective commands.

BY COMMAND OF MAJOR GENERAL HALLECK,

General-in-chief of the Army :

E. D. TOWNSEND,

Assistant Adjutant General.

GENERAL ORDERS, ⎫
No. 108. ⎭

WAR DEPARTMENT,
ADJUTANT GENERAL'S OFFICE,
Washington, August 16, 1862.

The following order of the President of the United States, dated August 14, 1862, is published for the information of all concerned :

ORDERED :

1st. That after the fifteenth of this month, bounty and advanced pay shall not be paid to Volunteers for any new regiments, but only to Volunteers for regiments now in the field and Volunteers to fill up new regiments now organizing but not yet full.

2d. Volunteers to fill up the new regiments now organizing will be received and paid the bounty and advanced pay until the twenty-second day of this month, and if not completed by that time, the incomplete regiments will be consolidated, and superfluous officers mustered out.

3d. Volunteers to fill up the old regiments will be received and paid the bounty and advance pay until the first day of September.

4th. The draft for three hundred thousand Militia, called for by the President, will be made on Wednesday, the third day of September, between the hours of 9 o'clock a. m. and 5 o'clock p. m., and continued from day to day, between the same hours, until completed.

5th. If the old regiments should not be filled up by Volunteers before the first day of September, a special draft will be ordered for the deficiency.

BY ORDER OF THE SECRETARY OF WAR:

E. D. TOWNSEND,
Assistant Adjutant General.

GENERAL ORDERS,
No. 109.

WAR DEPARTMENT,
ADJUTANT GENERAL'S OFFICE,
Washington, August 16, 1862.

The following is an order of the President of the United States, dated July 22, 1862:

First. Ordered, That military commanders within the States of Virginia, South Carolina, Georgia, Florida, Alabama, Mississippi, Louisiana, Texas, and Arkansas, in an orderly manner, seize and use any property, real or personal, which may be necessary or convenient for their several commands as supplies, or for other military purposes; and that, while property may be destroyed for proper military objects, none shall be destroyed in wantonness or malice.

106

Second. That military and naval commanders shall employ as laborers, within and from said States, so many persons of African descent as can be advantageously used for military and naval purposes, giving them reasonable wages for their labor.

Third. That, as to both property and persons of African descent, accounts shall be kept sufficiently accurate and in detail to show quantities and amounts, and from whom both property and such persons shall have come, as a basis upon which compensation can be made in proper cases ; and the several departments of this government shall attend to and perform their appropriate parts toward the execution of these orders.

BY ORDER OF THE SECRETARY OF WAR:

E. D. TOWNSEND,
Assistant Adjutant General.

GENERAL ORDERS, }   WAR DEPARTMENT,
ADJUTANT GENERAL'S OFFICE,
No. 111.   *Washington, August* 18, 1862.

I.. Hereafter no appointments of Major General or Brigadier General will be given, except to officers of the regular army for meritorious and distinguished services during the war, or to volunteer officers who, by some successful achievement in the field, shall have displayed the military abilities required for the duties of a general officer.

II.. No appointment to such grades will be issued by the War Department till an examination is made to ascertain if there are any charges or evidence against the character, conduct, or fitness of the appointee, and if there should be any such charges or evidence, a special report of the same will be made to the President.

BY ORDER OF THE SECRETARY OF WAR:

E. D. TOWNSEND,
Assistant Adjutant General.

GENERAL ORDERS, }   WAR DEPARTMENT,
ADJUTANT GENERAL'S OFFICE,
No. 113   *Washington, August* 20, 1862.

Detachments of recruits will be furnished with at least two days' cooked rations before starting from the depot for their regiments. If delayed in any city *en route*, a detachment will be marched to the "Soldier's Rest," where additional cooked rations will be issued to the men sufficient to last till their arrival at the next "Rest," or at the destination of the detachment, according to circumstances. Superintendents of the recruiting service for States or Districts will see that this order is executed.

The officers, or non-commissioned officers, in charge of detachments *en route*, are responsible that the rations are not wasted. Also that such as are required are obtained at the Rests. Purchases of articles of food on public account are not authorized.

By Order of the Secretary of War:

E. D. TOWNSEND,
Assistant Adjutant General.

GENERAL ORDERS,　　　　WAR DEPARTMENT,
　　　　　　　　　　　　　ADJUTANT GENERAL'S OFFICE,
No. 114.　　　　　　　　　*Washington, August 21, 1862.*

1..No officer of the regular army or of volunteers will hereafter visit the city of Washington without special permission. Leaves of absence will not be considered as including the city of Washington, unless so stated, and leaves for that purpose can only be given by the authority of the War Department, through the Adjutant General.

II..Officers on leave of absence will not leave the limits of their Military Department without special permission.

By Order of the Secretary of War:

E. D. TOWNSEND,
Assistant Adjutant General.

GENERAL ORDERS,　　　　WAR DEPARTMENT,
　　　　　　　　　　　　　ADJUTANT GENERAL'S OFFICE,
No. 116.　　　　　　　　　*Washington, August 23, 1862.*

I..Commissioned officers and enlisted men of the discharged three months' volunteer regiments who have been exchanged or released on parole by the enemy, and not yet discharged the United States service, are hereby mustered out and discharged from this date.

II..Officers and men of the forces aforesaid, who may hereafter be exchanged or released by the enemy, will be considered as regularly mustered out and discharged the service of the United States from the date of their arrival in a loyal State.

BY ORDER OF THE SECRETARY OF WAR:

E. D. TOWNSEND,

Assistant Adjutant General.

GENERAL ORDERS,   WAR DEPARTMENT,
                       ADJUTANT GENERAL'S OFFICE,
No. 118.   *Washington, August* 27, 1862.

I..The following partial list of officers of the United States service, who have been exchanged as prisoners of war, for prisoners taken in arms against the United States, is published for the information of all concerned :

o   o   o   o   o

IV..FEDERAL PRISONERS.—

Prisoners delivered at City Point, James river, nine lists, equivalent to 4,135 privates, received by Colonel Sweitzer, fully exchanged.

Hatteras delivery, to General Burnside, fully exchanged.

Fort Macon delivery, to General Burnside, fully exchanged.

Enlisted men captured at Murfreesboro', Tennessee, by General Forrest, fully exchanged.

Delivery of rank and file to Adjutant General U. S. Army, at Aiken's Landing, James river—upwards of 3,000—August 5, 1862, fully exchanged.

Generals Prentiss and Crittenden will be exchanged for Generals Mackall and Pettigrew, respectively, so soon as the two former, now in the West, are released ; the latter, in the meantime, being prisoners on parole.

BY ORDER OF THE SECRETARY OF WAR :

L. THOMAS,

Adjutant General.

GENERAL ORDERS,   WAR DEPARTMENT,
                      ADJUTANT GENERAL'S OFFICE,
No. 119.   .   *Washington, August* 29, 1862.

The following orders are published for the information and government of all concerned :

ORDER RESPECTING TRADE REGULATIONS.

WAR DEPARTMENT,
Washington City, D. C., August 28, 1862.

The attention of all officers and others connected with the Army of the United States is called to the Regulations of the Secretary of the Treasury concerning commercial intercourse with insurrectionary States, or sections, dated August 28, 1862.

I.--Commandants of Departments, Districts, and Posts, will render all such military aid as may become necessary in carrying out the provisions of said Regulations and enforcing observance thereof to the extent directed by the Secretary of the Treasury, so far as can possibly be done without danger to the operations or safety of their respective commands.

II.--There will be no interference with trade in, or shipments of, cotton, or other merchandise, conducted in pursuance of said Regulations, within any territory occupied and controlled by the forces of the United States, unless absolutely necessary to the successful execution of military plans or movements therein. But in cases of the violation of the conditions of any clearance or permit granted under said Regulations, and in cases of unlawful traffic, the guilty party or parties will be arrested and the facts promptly reported to the commandant of the department for orders.

III.--No officer of the Army, or other person connected therewith, will seize cotton, or other property of individuals, unless exposed to destruction by the enemy, or needed for military purposes, or for confiscation under the act of Congress ; and in all such cases of seizure the same shall be promptly reported to the commandant of the Department wherein they are made for his orders therein.

BY ORDER OF THE SECRETARY OF WAR:

E. D. TOWNSEND,
Assistant Adjutant General.

110

GENERAL ORDERS,   WAR DEPARTMENT,
                 ADJUTANT GENERAL'S OFFICE,

No. 121.   *Washington, August* 29, 1862.

ORDER CONCERNING SUPPLIES TO DRAFTED MILITIA.

The commissioners for drafting in each county will, on the assembling of the draft at the county seat, appoint a lance corporal for every eight men, and a lance sergeant for every sixteen men, and will make fair and reasonable contracts for cooked provisions sufficient to subsist the men until their arrival at the camp of rendezvous and twenty-four hours thereafter; copies of these contracts, and duplicate bills, certified by the commissioner and by the mustering officer, will be sent to the Commissary General for payment.

The commissioner will accompany the men to the camp, taking the control of them, providing for their transportation by railroad or steamboat when practicable, and, where it is necessary to march, he may provide a reasonable amount of transportation for the provisions and baggage of the men. The expenses of transportation will be paid by the Quartermaster's Department on duplicate bills, certified by the commissioner.

The chief mustering officer of each State will immediately, in conformity with the regulations of the Subsistence Department, advertise for separate proposals, and make contracts for uncooked rations for each camp, and will also immediately make their requisitions on the Commissary General for funds to meet all subsistence for drafted men, while they remain in camp of rendezvous.

Until companies are organized, the rations will be supplied on the returns of the commander of each camp, and his receipt will be the basis for a settlement with the contractor.

After organization into companies, rations will be issued on returns signed by the company commanders, and approved by the commandant of the camp.

After being organized into regiments, rations will be supplied to the Regimental Quartermaster on regimental returns signed by him, and approved by the Colonel—the Regimental Quartermaster being charged with their distribution to the companies.

Cooking utensils, and such other camp equipage and blankets as can be furnished by the Quartermaster's Department, will be supplied as soon as possible by the United States Quartermasters hereinafter named, on the requisitions of the commandants of camps of rendezvous within their respective districts, and will be issued by such commandants to the men, as follows: Each man receiving a blanket will receipt for the same, which receipt will be turned over by the commandant of the camp of rendezvous to the quartermaster of his regiment, as soon as he shall be appointed, and he shall make the proper entry on his account.

Camp equipage issued before the organization of companies will be receipted for by the lance sergeant of the squad, and taken up by the quartermaster of the regiment, on his return, as soon as the regiment is organized. When issued after the organization of a company, it will be receipted for by the captain, and taken up in like manner.

It will be the duty of the officer of the United States Quartermaster's Department to forward to the several camps of rendezvous, as soon as possible, camp and garrison equipage, necessary for the first organization. Arrangements now in progress will provide the uniform clothing, which will not be issued to the soldiers until the organization of regiments is completed.

As the sudden call for volunteers and militia has exhausted the supply of blankets, fit for military purposes, in the market, and it will take some time to procure by manufacture or importation a sufficient supply, all citizens who may volunteer or be drafted are advised to take with them to the rendezvous, if possible, a good, stout woolen blanket. The regulation military blanket is 84 x 66 inches, and weighs five pounds.

As all clothing, blankets, and shoes issued by the United States to its troops are charged at average cost, and no soldier who furnishes his own blanket is required to draw one, it is to his interest to supply himself, and thereby avoid much discomfort, as it is impossible for the United States to supply all the troops immediately.

The camps of rendezvous in the different States will be supplied by the United States Quartermaster as follows: Camps in

Maine, New Hampshire, Massachusetts,	Captain McKim, Assistant Q. M., Boston.
Vermont, Connecticut, Rhode Island, New York, New Jersey, (part of,)	Colonel Vinton, Deputy Q. M. G., New York.
New Jersey, (part of,) Pennsylvania, Delaware,	Colonel Crosman, Deputy Q. M. G., Philadelphia.

Camps near Harrisburg will be supplied by requisition upon Captain E. C. Wilson, A. Q. M., at Harrisburg. Those near Pittsburg by Major A. Montgomery, Q. M., U. S. A., at Pittsburg.

Ohio—Captain J. H. Dickerson, A. Q. M , Cincinnati.

Indiana—Captain James A. E. Kin, A. Q. M., Indianapolis.

Illinois,
Wisconsin, Captain J. A. Potter, A. Q. M.,
Chicago.

Kentucky—Colonel Thomas Swords, A. Q. M. Gen'l, Louisville.

Michigan—Captain G. W. Lee, A. Q. M., Detroit.

Iowa—Captain H. B. Hendershott, 2d Artillery, Davenport.

Minnesota—Captain T. M. Saunders, 3d Artillery, St. Paul.

Camps near St. Louis will be supplied by Major Robert Allen, Chief Quartermaster of the Department of the Mississippi.

By order of the Secretary of War:

E. D. TOWNSEND,
Assistant Adjutant General.

GENERAL ORDERS, }
No. 126. }

WAR DEPARTMENT,
Adjutant General's Office,
Washington, September 6, 1862.

I..The following is the organization of Regiments and Companies of the Volunteer Army of the United States:

1. Regiment of Infantry—*Ten Companies..*

1 Colonel.

1 Lieutenant Colonel.

1 Major.

1 Adjutant, (an extra Lieut.)

1 Quartermaster, (an extra Lieut.)
1 Surgeon.
2 Assistant Surgeons.
1 Chaplain.
1 Sergeant Major.

1 Regimental Quartermaster Sergeant.
1 Regimental Commissary Sergeant.
1 Hospital Steward.

Company of Infantry.

1 Captain.
1 First Lieutenant.
1 Second Lieutenant.
1 First Sergeant.

4 Sergeants.
8 Corporals.
2 Musicians.
1 Wagoner.

And $\begin{cases} 64 \text{ Privates—minimum.} \\ 82 \text{ Privates—maximum.} \end{cases}$

2. REGIMENT OF CAVALRY—*Twelve Companies or Troops.*

1 Colonel.
1 Lieutenant Colonel.
3 Majors.
1 Surgeon.
1 Assistant Surgeon.
1 Regimental Adjutant, (an extra Lieut)
1 Regimental Quartermaster, (an extra Lieut.)

1 Regimental Commissary, (an extra Lieut.)
1 Chaplain.
1 Sergeant Major.
1 Quartermaster Sergeant.
1 Commissary Sergeant.
2 Hospital Stewards.
1 Saddler Sergeant.
1 Chief Farrier or Blacksmith.

Company or Troop of Cavalry.

1 Captain.
1 First Lieutenant.
1 Second Lieutenant.
1 First Sergeant.
1 Quartermaster Sergeant.
1 Commissary Sergeant.
5 Sergeants.

8 Corporals.
2 Teamsters.
2 Farriers or Blacksmiths.
1 Saddler.
1 Wagoner, and
78 Privates.

There being no bands now allowed, the chief trumpeter authorized

8

by law will not be mustered into service. If any have been so mustered, they will, upon receipt of this order, be mustered out.

The law does not authorize *musicians for companies.* To remedy this defect, two musicians may be enlisted for each company. *They will be rated and paid as privates.*

3. REGIMENT OF ARTILLERY—*Twelve Batteries.*

1 Colonel.	1 Chaplain.
1 Lieutenant Colonel.	1 Sergeant Major.
1 Major for every four batteries.	1 Quartermaster Sergeant.
1 Adjutant, (not an extra Lieut.)	1 Commissary Sergeant.
1 Quartermaster, (not an extra Lieut.)	1 Hospital Steward.

Battery of Artillery.

1 Captain.	8 Corporals.
1 First Lieutenant.	2 Musicians.
1 Second Lieutenant.	2 Artificers.
1 First Sergeant.	1 Wagoner, and
1 Quartermaster Sergeant.	122 Privates.
4 Sergeants.	

To the above organization of a battery, one First and one Second Lieutenant, two Sergeants, and four Corporals may be added, at the President's discretion.

The field officers, chaplain, and regimental staff—commissioned and non-commissioned—will not be mustered, or received, into service, without special authority from the War Department. As a general rule, Artillery will be called for, and received, by batteries, thus rendering the field and staff unnecessary.

II..Chaplains must meet the requirements of section 8 of the act of July 17, 1862, as follows:

"No person shall be appointed a chaplain in the United States Army who is not a regularly ordained minister of some religious denomination, and who does not present testimonials of his present good standing as such minister, with a recommendation for his appointment as an Army chaplain from some authorized ecclesiastical body, or not less than five accredited ministers belonging to said religious denomination."

After Chaplains are appointed, under section 9, of the act of July 22, 1861, they must be mustered into service by an officer of the regular army, and thereafter borne on the field and staff roll of the regiment.

Mustering officers, before mustering Chaplains into service, will require from them a copy of the proceedings on which the appointment is based. The said copy, if found conformable to the requirements of the law, will be indorsed by the mustering officer, and by him forwarded to the Adjutant General's office, for file with the muster-in roll.

III..The foregoing organization must be strictly adhered to by all concerned. Commanding Officers of Departments, Armies, and Army Corps, will, without delay, direct an inspection to be made of their commands, to ascertain if the *regiments, and units thereof*, conform to this organization, and all deviation from it will be promptly corrected. Supernumerary officers, if any, will be mustered out of service from the date of receipt of this order. Reports of the inspection will be forwarded to the Adjutant General of the Army.

No commissioned officer or enlisted man, of any grade, in excess of the legal organization, will be recognized. And any commander who may acknowledge, or receive, as in service, any such officer or enlisted man, will be brought to trial for neglect of duty and disobedience of orders. No person acting in the capacity of a supernumerary will, under any circumstances, be permitted to receive pay and allowances from the government; and Paymasters making payment to such supernumeraries will be held individually accountable for amounts so paid.

By order of the Secretary of War :

L. THOMAS,
Adjutant General.

116

GENERAL ORDERS,   WAR DEPARTMENT,
                                    ADJUTANT GENERAL'S OFFICE.
No. 130.   *Washington, September* 14, 1862.

I..The attention of all officers, and especially of commanders of Departments and Army Corps, is called to the absolute necessity of reducing the baggage trains of troops in the field. The mobility of our armies is destroyed by the vast trains which attend them, and which they are required to guard. This evil requires a prompt remedy. Officers will hereafter be allowed to carry into the field only the ordinary mess chest and a valise or carpet bag. No trunks or boxes will be permitted in the baggage trains. Privates frequently carry carpet bags and boxes in the regimental wagons. This must be immediately stopped. Inspectors, quartermasters, and wagonmasters will see that such articles are ejected from the wagons and cars wherever found; and regimental and company officers who permit these abuses will be reported, through the proper channels, for dismissal from service. Commanders of Departments and Army Corps will direct frequent inspections to be made of baggage trains, and especially of officers' baggage, and see that this order is strictly enforced in their respective commands.

II..Another cause of the increase of trains is the carrying of sutlers' goods in regimental or quartermaster wagons, under the guise of quartermaster and commissary stores. Hereafter, any officer or wagonmaster who permits this abuse will be duly punished, and the sutler whose goods are so carried will be placed without the lines of the army, and his appointment revoked.

BY COMMAND OF MAJOR GENERAL HALLECK:

L. THOMAS,
Adjutant General.

GENERAL ORDERS,   WAR DEPARTMENT,
                                    ADJUTANT GENERAL'S OFFICE,
No. 132.   *Washington, September* 17, 1862.

1..*Ordered,* That Medical Purveyors be required to give bond in the sum of seventy-five thousand dollars.

II..The following Regulations have been adopted to govern the allowances to officers under sections 1 and 2, Act of July 17, 1862, "To define the pay and emoluments of certain officers of the Army:"

1. When forage in kind cannot be furnished by the proper department, officers entitled to forage may commute it for the number of horses specified in section 2, upon the certificate of the quartermaster, when there is one, or of the commanding officer, when there is no quartermaster, that forage in kind cannot be furnished. When the officer is on detached duty, his own certificate to the fact, with the additional statement that there is no commanding officer or quartermaster serving with him, will entitle him to the commutation.

2. Officers on leave of absence are not entitled to forage, or to commutation therefor.

3. Officers of the Army and of Volunteers detailed for duty in the Engineers or other branches of the staff, are not, as a matter of course, entitled to the pay, emoluments, and allowances of cavalry officers. But, when ordered by the proper authority to be mounted, and when so mounted at their own expense, they are entitled.

By Order of the Secretary of War:

L THOMAS,
Adjutant General.

GENERAL ORDERS,	WAR DEPARTMENT,
	Adjutant General's Office,
No. 134.	*Washington, September* 19, 1862.

The prisoners of war, except commissioned officers, who were delivered to Lieutenant Colonel Ludlow, Aide-de-Camp to Major General Dix, at Aiken's Landing, James river, Virginia, on the 14th and 15th instant, are declared to be exchanged.

By Order of the Secretary of War:

L. THOMAS,
Adjutant General.

118

GENERAL ORDERS,   WAR DEPARTMENT,
                          ADJUTANT GENERAL'S OFFICE,
No. 139.   *Washington, September* 24, 1862.

The following proclamation by the President is published for the information and government of the Army and all concerned:

BY THE PRESIDENT OF THE UNITED STATES OF AMERICA.

A PROCLAMATION.

I, ABRAHAM LINCOLN, President of the United States of America, and Commander-in-Chief of the Army and Navy thereof, do hereby proclaim and declare that hereafter, as heretofore, the war will be prosecuted for the object of practically restoring the constitutional relation between the United States and each of the States, and the people thereof, in which States that relation is or may be suspended or disturbed.

That it is my purpose, upon the next meeting of Congress, to again recommend the adoption of a practical measure tending pecuniary aid to the free acceptance or rejection of all Slave States, so called, the people whereof may not then be in rebellion against the United States, and which States may then have voluntarily adopted, or thereafter may voluntarily adopt, immediate or gradual abolishment of slavery within their respective limits; and that the effort to colonize persons of African descent, with their consent, upon this continent or elsewhere, with the previously obtained consent of the governments existing there, will be continued.

That on the first day of January, in the year of our Lord one thousand eight hundred and sixty-three, all persons held as slaves within any State or designated part of a State, the people whereof shall then be in rebellion against the United States, shall be then, thenceforward, and forever free; and the Executive Government of the United States, including the military and naval authority thereof, will recognize and maintain the freedom of such persons, and will do no act or acts to repress such persons, or any of them, in any efforts they may make for their actual freedom.

That the Executive will, on the first day of January aforesaid, by proclamation, designate the States, and parts of States, if any, in which the people thereof respectively shall then be in rebellion against the United States; and the fact that any State, or the people thereof, shall on that day be in good faith represented in the Congress of the United States, by members chosen thereto at elections wherein a majority of the qualified voters of such State shall have participated, shall, in the absence of strong countervailing testimony, be deemed conclusive evidence that such State, and the people thereof, are not then in rebellion against the United States.

.That attention is hereby called to an act of Congress entitled "An act to make an additional Article of War," approved March 13, 1862, and which act is in the words and figures following :

"*Be it enacted by the Senate and House of Representatives of the United States of America in Congress assembled,* That hereafter the following hall be promulgated as an additional article of war for the government of the Army of the United States, and shall be obeyed and observed as such :

"ARTICLE —. All officers or persons in the military or naval service of the United States are prohibited from employing any of the forces under their respective commands for the purpose of returning fugitives from service or labor who may have escaped from any person to whom such service or labor is claimed to be due; and any officer who shall be found guilty by a court-martial of violating this article, shall be dismissed from the service.

"SEC. 2. *And be it further enacted,* That this act shall take effect from and after its passage."

Also, to the ninth and tenth sections of an act entitled "An act to suppress insurrection, to punish treason and rebellion, to seize and confiscate property of rebels, and for other purposes," approved July 17, 1862, and which sections are in the words and figures following :

SEC. 9. *And be it further enacted,* That all slaves of persons who shall hereafter be engaged in rebellion against the govvernment of the United States, or who shall in any way give aid or comfort thereto, escaping from such persons and taking refuge within the lines of the army ; and all slaves captured from such persons, or deserted by them and coming under the control of the government of the United States ; and all slaves of such persons found *on* [or] being within any place occupied by rebel forces and afterwards occupied by the forces of the United States, shall be deemed captives of war, and shall be forever free of their servitude, and not again held as slaves.

"Sec. 10. *And be it further enacted,* That no slave escaping into any State, Territory, or the District of Columbia, from any other State, shall be delivered up, or in any way impeded or hindered of his liberty, except for crime, or some offence against the laws, unless the person claiming said fugitive shall first make oath that the person to whom the labor or service of such fugitive is alleged to be due is his lawful owner, and has not borne arms against the United States in the present rebellion, nor in any way given aid and comfort thereto ; and no person engaged in the military or naval service of the United States shall, under any pretence whatever, assume to decide on the validity of the claim of any person to the service or labor of any other person, or surrender up any such person to the claimant, on pain of being dismissed from the service."

And I do hereby enjoin upon and order all persons engaged in the military and naval service of the United States to observe, obey, and enforce, within their respective spheres of service, the act and sections above recited.

And the Executive will in due time recommend that all citizens of the United States who shall have remained loyal thereto throughout the rebellion shall (upon the restoration of the constitutional relation between the United States and their respective States and people, if that relation shall have been suspended or disturbed) be compensated for all losses by acts of the United States, including the loss of slaves.

In witness whereof, I have hereunto set my hand and caused the seal of the United States to be affixed.

Done at the City of Washington, this twenty-second day of September, in the year of our Lord one thousand eight hundred and

[SEAL.]   sixty-two, and of the Independence of the United States
the eighty-seventh.

ABRAHAM LINCOLN.

By the President:

WILLIAM H. SEWARD, *Secretary of State.*

BY ORDER OF THE SECRETARY OF WAR :

L. THOMAS,

Adjutant General.

GENERAL ORDERS,	WAR DEPARTMENT,
No. 140.	ADJUTANT GENERAL'S OFFICE, *Washington, September 24, 1862.*

ORDER *respecting Special Provost Marshals, and defining their duties.*

First. There shall be a Provost Marshal General of the War Department, whose headquarters will be at Washington, and who will have the immediate supervision, control, and management of the corps.

Second. There will be appointed in each State one or more Special Provost Marshals, as necessity may require, who will report to, and receive instructions and orders from, the Provost Marshal General of the War Department.

Third. It will be the duty of the Special Provost Marshals to arrest all deserters, whether Regulars, Volunteers, or Militia, and send them to the nearest Military Commander, or military post, where they can be cared for and sent to their respective Regiments ; to arrest, upon the warrant of the Judge Advocate, all disloyal persons subject to arrest under the orders of the War Department ; to inquire into and report treasonable practices, seize stolen or embezzled property of the government, detect spies of the enemy, and perform such other duties as may be enjoined upon them by the War Department ; and report all their proceedings promptly to the Provost Marshal General.

Fourth. To enable Special Provost Marshals to discharge their duties efficiently, they are authorized to call on any available military force within their respective districts, or else to employ the assistance of citizens, constables, sheriffs, or police officers, so far as may be necessary, under such regulations as may be prescribed by the Provost

Marshal General of the War Department, with the approval of the Secretary of War.

Fifth. Necessary expenses incurred in this service will be paid on duplicate bills certified by the Special Provost Marshals stating the time and nature of the service, after examination and approval by the Provost Marshal General.

Sixth. The compensation of Special Provost Marshals will be   dollars per month, and actual travelling expenses and postage will be refunded on bills certified under oath and approved by the Provost Marshal General.

Seventh. All appointments in this service will be subject to be revoked at the pleasure of the Secretary of War.

Eighth. All orders heretofore issued by the War Department conferring authority upon other officers to act as Provost Marshals (except those who have received special commissions from the War Department) are hereby revoked.

BY ORDER OF THE SECRETARY OF WAR:

L. THOMAS,
Adjutant General.

GENERAL ORDERS,   }   WAR DEPARTMENT,
                     }   ADJUTANT GENERAL'S OFFICE,
No. 141.   }   *Washington, September* 25, 1862.

The following Proclamation by the President is published for the information and government of the Army and all concerned:

BY THE PRESIDENT OF THE UNITED STATES OF AMERICA.

A PROCLAMATION.

WHEREAS it has become necessary to call into service not only Volunteers but also portions of the Militia of the States by draft, in order to suppress the insurrection existing in the United States, and disloyal persons are not adequately restrained by the ordinary processes of law from hindering this measure and from giving aid and comfort in various ways to the insurrection:

Now, therefore, be it ordered—

First. That during the existing insurrection, and as a necessary measure for suppressing the same, all rebels and insurgents, their aiders and abettors, within the United States, and all persons discouraging volunteer enlistments, resisting militia drafts, or guilty of any disloyal practice, affording aid and comfort to rebels against the authority of the United States, shall be subject to martial law, and liable to trial and punishment by courts-martial or military commission.

Second. That the writ of habeas corpus is suspended in respect to all persons arrested, or who are now, or hereafter during the rebellion shall be, imprisoned in any fort, camp, arsenal, military prison, or other place of confinement by any military authority, or by the sentence of any court-martial or military commission.

In witness whereof, I have hereunto set my hand, and caused the seal of the United States to be affixed.

Done at the city of Washington, this twenty-fourth day of September, in the year of our Lord one thousand eight hundred [L. S.] and sixty-two, and of the Independence of the United States the eighty-seventh.

ABRAHAM LINCOLN.

By the President:
WILLIAM H. SEWARD,
Secretary of State.

BY ORDER OF THE SECRETARY OF WAR:

L. THOMAS,
Adjutant General.

GENERAL ORDERS,
No. 142.

WAR DEPARTMENT,
ADJUTANT GENERAL'S OFFICE,
Washington, Sept. 25, 1862.

The following is the cartel under which prisoners are exchanged in the existing war with the Southern States:

HAXALL'S LANDING ON JAMES RIVER, VA.,
July 22, 1862.

The undersigned, having been commissioned by the authorities they respectively represent to make arrangements for a general exchange of prisoners of war, have agreed to the following articles :

Article 1. It is hereby agreed and stipulated that all prisoners of war held by either party, including those taken on private armed vessels known as privateers, shall be discharged upon the conditions and terms following :

Prisoners to be exchanged man for man and officer for officer; privateers to be placed upon the footing of officers and men of the Navy.

Men and officers of lower grades may be exchanged for officers of a higher grade, and men and officers of different services may be exchanged according to the following scale of equivalents :

A General commanding in chief or an Admiral shall be exchanged for officers of equal rank or for sixty privates or common seamen.

A Flag Officer or Major General shall be exchanged for officers of equal rank or for forty privates or common seamen.

A Commodore carrying a broad pennant or a Brigadier General shall be exchanged for officers of equal rank or twenty privates or common seamen.

A Captain in the Navy or a Colonel shall be exchanged for officers of equal rank or for fifteen privates or common seamen

A Lieutenant Colonel or a Commander in the Navy shall be exchanged for officers of equal rank or for ten privates or common seamen.

A Lieutenant Commander or a Major shall be exchanged for officers of equal rank or eight privates or common seamen.

A Lieutenant or a master in the Navy or a Captain in the Army or Marines shall be exchanged for officers of equal rank or six privates or common seamen.

Master's Mates in the Navy or Lieutenants and Ensigns in the Army shall be exchanged for officers of equal rank or four privates or common seamen.

Midshipmen, Warrant Officers in the Navy, Masters of merchant vessels, and Commanders of privateers shall be exchanged for officers of equal rank or three privates or common seamen.

Second Captains, Lieutenants, or Mates of merchant vessels or privateers, and all petty officers in the Navy and all non-commissioned officers in the Army or Marines, shall be severally exchanged for persons of equal rank or for two privates or common seamen; and private soldiers or common seamen shall be exchanged for each other man for man.

Article 2. Local, State, civil, and militia rank held by persons not in actual military service will not be recognized, the basis of exchange being the grade actually held in the naval and military service of the respective parties.

Article 3. If citizens held by either party on charge of disloyalty or any alleged civil offence are exchanged, it shall only be for citizens. Captured sutlers, teamsters, and all civilians in the actual service of either party, to be exchanged for persons in similar position.

Article 4. All prisoners of war to be discharged on parole in ten days after their capture, and the prisoners now held and those hereafter taken to be transported to the points mutually agreed upon, at the expense of the capturing party. The surplus prisoners not exchanged shall not be permitted to take up arms again, nor to serve as military police or constabulary force in any fort, garrison, or field work held by either of the respective parties, nor as guards of prisons, depots, or stores, nor to discharge any duty usually performed by soldiers, until exchanged under the provisions of this cartel. The exchange is not to be considered complete until the officer or soldier exchanged for has been actually restored to the lines to which he belongs.

Article 5. Each party, upon the discharge of prisoners of the other party, is authorized to discharge an equal number of their own officers or men from parole, furnishing at the same time to the other party a list of their prisoners discharged and of their own officers and men relieved from parole; thus enabling each party to relieve from parole such of their own officers and men as the party may choose. The lists thus mutually furnished will keep both parties advised of the true condition of the exchange of prisoners.

Article 6. The stipulations and provisions above mentioned to be of binding obligation during the continuance of the war, it matters not which party may have the surplus of prisoners, the great principles involved being—1st. An equitable exchange of prisoners, man for man, officer for officer, or officers of higher grade exchanged for officers of lower grade, or for privates, according to the scale of equivalents; 2d. That privateers and officers and men of different services may be exchanged according to the same scale of equivalents; 3d. That all prisoners, of whatever arm of service, are to be exchanged or paroled in ten days from the time of their capture, if it be practicable to transfer them to their own lines in that time ; if not, as soon thereafter as practicable ; 4th. That no officer, soldier, or employé in the service of either party is to be considered as exchanged and absolved from his parole until his equivalent has actually reached the lines of his friends ; 5th. That the parole forbids the performance of field, garrison, police, or guard, or constabulary duty.

(Signed) JOHN A. DIX,
       Major General.
(Signed) D. H. HILL,
    Major General C. S. A.

SUPPLEMENTARY ARTICLES.

Article 7. All prisoners of war now held on either side, and all prisoners hereafter taken, shall be sent with all reasonable despatch to A. M. Aikens', below Dutch Gap, on the James river, Virginia, or to Vicksburg, on the Mississippi river, in the State of Mississippi, and there exchanged or paroled until such exchange can be effected, notice being previously given by each party of the number of prisoners it will send, and the time when they will be delivered at those points respectively; and in case the vicissitudes of war shall change the military relations of the places designated in this article to the contending parties so as to render the same inconvenient for the delivery and exchange of prisoners, other places, bearing as nearly as may be the present local relations of said places to the lines of said parties, shall be by mutual agreement substituted. But nothing in this article contained shall prevent the commanders of two opposing armies from exchanging prisoners or releasing them on parole at other points mutually agreed on by said commanders.

Article 8. For the purpose of carrying into effect the foregoing articles of agreement, each party will appoint two agents, to be called Agents for the exchange of prisoners of war, whose duty it shall be to communicate with each other, by correspondence and otherwise, and prepare the lists of prisoners, to attend to the delivery of the prisoners at the places agreed on, and to carry out promptly, effectually, and in good faith, all the details and provisions of the said articles of agreement.

Article 9. And in case any misunderstanding shall arise in regard to any clause or stipulation in the foregoing articles, it is mutually agreed that such misunderstanding shall not interrupt the release of prisoners on parole, as herein provided, but shall be made the subject of friendly explanations, in order that the object of this agreement may neither be defeated nor postponed.

(Signed)   JOHN A. DIX,
Major General.

(Signed)   D. H. HILL,
Major General C. S. A.

By order of the Secretary of War :

L. THOMAS,
Adjutant General.

GENERAL ORDERS, }   WAR DEPARTMENT,
ADJUTANT GENERAL's OFFICE,
No. 145. }   *Washington, September* 29, 1862.

I..The Department is informed that certain general officers of the Volunteer Service, on being relieved from their commands, or transferred from one command to another, have occasionally carried off with them the soldiers employed as clerks or orderlies at their former headquarters. Not only had they no right and should have known better than to do so, but it was wrong in their superiors in command to permit it ; nor will it again be permitted.

II..All soldiers so separated from their regiments will be immediately returned to them ; and the commanding officers of all regiments, from which men are thus irregularly detached, shall, if the latter be not returned within a reasonable time, promptly report the facts to this office, for the further action of the Department.

BY ORDER OF THE SECRETARY OF WAR :

L. THOMAS,
Adjutant General.

GENERAL ORDERS. }   WAR DEPARTMENT,
ADJUTANT GENERAL'S OFFICE,
No. 146. }   *Washington, September* 30, 1862.

No officer will hereafter be relieved from his command and sent to report in this city without the authority of the War Department. Where subordinate officers are guilty of military offences, or are negligent, or incompetent, it is the duty of the Commander to have them tried for their offences, or examined in regard to their incompetency, by a proper court or commission ; and this duty cannot be evaded by sending them to Washington. Hereafter, officers so sent to Headquarters will be immediately ordered back, and those who send them will be deemed guilty of disobedience of orders.

BY COMMAND OF MAJOR GENERAL HALLECK :

L. THOMAS,
Adjutant General.

GENERAL ORDERS, }   WAR DEPARTMENT,
ADJUTANT GENERAL'S OFFICE,
No. 147. }   *Washington, September* 30, 1862.

The following lists of officers of the United States service who have been exchanged as prisoners of War, September 21, 1862, at Aiken's Landing, Virginia, for prisoners taken in arms against the United States, are published for the information of all concerned :

IV.--FEDERAL PRISONERS.

The following is a list of exchanges which have been made since the lists already published :

Delivered to Lieutenant Colonel Ludlow, at Aiken's Landing,
September 7, 1862..716
Delivered to Lieutenant Colonel Ludlow, at Aiken's Landing,
September 21, 1862..334
Private William Seymour, 2d U. S. Infantry.

1st U. S. infantry......	⎫	114
3d U. S. Infantry.......	⎬ Texas Exchange.	231
8th U. S. Infantry......	⎭	182
3d U. S. Cavalry........	⎫ New Mexico Exchange.	98
7th U. S. Cavalry.......	⎭	459

Shiloh prisoners 2,001
Gainesville prisoners delivered to Major C. E. Livingston,
September 1, 1862...1,310
Gainesville prisoners delivered to Lieutenant D. S. Unckle,
August 30, 1862..271
The total number of exchanges to be offset by delivery of
Confederate prisoners at Vicksburg is now.............10,368

By ORDER OF THE SECRETARY OF WAR :

L. THOMAS,
Adjutant General.

GENERAL ORDERS, ⎫	WAR DEPARTMENT,
⎬	ADJUTANT GENERAL'S OFFICE,
No. 149. ⎭	*Washington, October* 2, 1862.

No person shall be mustered into the service of the United States as
a member of the Corps of Sharpshooters, unless he shall produce the
certificate of some person duly authorized by the Governor of the
State in which the company is raised, that he has in five consecutive
shots, at two hundred yards at rest, made a string not over twenty-five
inches ; or the same string off-hand at one hundred yards ; the certificate to be written on the target used at the test.

By ORDER OF THE SECRETARY OF WAR :

L. THOMAS,
Adjutant General.

9

GENERAL ORDERS,   WAR DEPARTMENT,
                   ADJUTANT'S GENERAL'S OFFICE,
No. 151.   *Washington, October* 4, 1862.

o   o   o   o   o   o   o   o

II..If any officer shall hereafter, without proper authority, permit the publication of any official letter or report, or allow any copy of such document to pass into the hands of persons not authorized to receive it, his name will be submitted to the President for dismissal. This rule applies to all official letters and reports written by an officer himself.

BY ORDER OF THE SECRETARY OF WAR :

L. THOMAS,
Adjutant General.

___

GENERAL ORDERS,   WAR DEPARTMENT,
                   ADJUTANT GENERAL'S OFFICE,
No. 152.   *Washington, October* 6, 1862.

The attention of all officers commanding *posts, districts,* or *brigades of troops,* to which *Chaplains* are attached, is again directed to sections 8 and 9 of the act "to define the pay and emoluments of certain officers of the Army," &c., approved July 17, 1862, and to the duty therein enjoined on them—a duty which they will at once fulfil.

The two sections of this law, referred to, though already published in General Orders, No. 91, of July 29, 1862, are republished for their information :

SEC. 8. *And be it further enacted,* That so much of section nine of the aforesaid act, approved July twenty-second, eighteen hundred and sixty-one, and of section seven of the "Act providing for the better organization of the military establishment," approved August third, eighteen hundred and sixty-one, as defines the qualifications of Chaplains in the Army and volunteers, shall hereafter be construed to read as follows: That no person shall be appointed a Chaplain in the United States Army who *is not a regularly ordained minister of some religious denomination, and who does not present testimonials of his present good standing as such minister, with a recommendation for his appointment as an Army Chaplain from some authorized ecclesiastical body, or not less than five accredited ministers belonging to said religious denomination.*

Sec. 9. *And be it further enacted,* That hereafter the compensation of all Chaplains in the regular or volunteer service or army hospitals shall be one hundred dollars per month and two rations a day when on duty; and the Chaplains of the permanent hospitals, appointed under the authority of the second section of the act approved May twentieth, eighteen hundred and sixty-two, shall be nominated to the Senate for its advice and consent, and they shall, in all respects, fill the requirements of the preceding section of this act relative to the appointment of Chaplains in the army and volunteers, and the appointments of Chaplains to army hospitals, heretofore made by the President, are hereby confirmed; *and it is hereby made the duty of each officer commanding a district or post containing hospitals, or a brigade of troops, within thirty days after the reception of the order promulgating this act, to inquire into the fitness, efficiency, and qualifications of the Chaplains of hospitals or regiments, and to muster out of service such Chaplains as were not appointed in conformity with the requirements of this act, and who have not faithfully discharged the duties of Chaplains during the time they have been engaged as such.*

Chaplains employed at the military posts called "Chaplains' posts" shall be required to reside at the posts, and all Chaplains in the United States service shall be subject to such rules in relation to leave of absence from duty as are prescribed for commissioned officers of the United States army stationed at such posts.

By order of the Secretary of War:

L. THOMAS,
Adjutant General.

GENERAL ORDERS, }
No. 154. }

WAR DEPARTMENT,
ADJUTANT GENERAL'S OFFICE,
Washington, October 9, 1862.

The commanding officer of each regiment, battalion, and battery of the Regular Army in the field, will appoint one or more recruiting officers, who are hereby authorized to enlist, with their own consent, the requisite number of efficient volunteers to fill the ranks of their command to the legal standard.

The enlistments will be made in the usual mode, and for three years, or for the remaining portion of the period of three years which the volunteer has yet to serve, if he so prefer.

The recruiting officers will furnish to the commanding officers of companies to which volunteers whom they may enlist belong, lists of such volunteers, exhibiting the dates of enlistment of each in the Regular Service. All the men upon such lists will be reported as honorably discharged the day previous to the date of their enlistment, on the first subsequent muster roll of their company.

As an inducement to volunteers to enlist in the Regular Army, it will be remembered that promotion to commissions therein is open by law to its meritorious and distinguished non-commissioned officers; and that many have already been promoted.

BY ORDER OF THE SECRETARY OF WAR:

L. THOMAS,
Adjutant General.

GENERAL ORDERS, }
No. 160. }

WAR DEPARTMENT,
ADJUTANT GENERAL'S OFFICE,
Washington, October 18, 1862.

The following regulations are established for Army Trains and Baggage :

I..There will be allowed—

For headquarters' train of an Army Corps, *four* wagons; of a Division or Brigade, *three;* of a full Infantry Regiment, *six;* and of a Light Artillery Battery or Squadron of Cavalry, *three.*

In no case will this allowance be exceeded, but always proportionably reduced according to the number of officers and men actually present. All surplus wagons will be turned over to the Chief Quartermaster to be organized, under direction of the Commanding Generals, into supply trains, or sent to the nearest depot.

The requisite supply trains, their size depending upon the state of the roads and character of the campaign, will be organized by the Chief Quartermaster, with the approval of the Commanding Generals, subject to the control of the War Department.

II..The wagons allowed to a regiment, battery, or squadron, must carry nothing but forage for the teams, cooking utensils, and rations for the troops, hospital stores, and officers' baggage. One wagon to each regiment will transport exclusively hospital supplies, under the direction of the Regimental Surgeon ; the one for regimental headquarters will carry the grain for the officers' horses ; and the three allowed for each battery or squadron, will be at least half loaded with grain for their own teams.

Stores in bulk and ammunition will be carried in the regular or special supply trains.

III..In active campaign, troops must be prepared to bivouac on the march, the allowance of tents, being limited, as follows:

For the headquarters of an Army Corps, Division, or Brigade, one wall tent to the Commanding General, and one to every two officers of his staff.

For the Colonel, Field, and Staff of a full regiment, three wall tents; and for every other commissioned officer, one shelter tent each.

For every two non-commissioned officers, soldiers, officers' servants, and authorized camp followers, one shelter tent.

One hospital tent will be allowed for office purposes at Corps headquarters, and one wall tent at those of a Division or a Brigade. All tents beyond this allowance will be left in depot.

IV..Officers' baggage will be limited to blankets, one small valise or carpet-bag, and a moderate mess-kit. The men will carry their own blankets and shelter tents, and reduce the contents of their knapsacks as much as possible.

The Depot. Quartermaster will provide storage for a reasonable amount of officers' surplus baggage, and the extra clothing and knapsacks of the men.

V..Hospital tents are for the sick and wounded, and, except those allowed for Army Corps headquarters, must not be diverted from their proper use.

VI..Commanding officers will be held responsible for the strict enforcement of these regulations, especially the reduction of officers' baggage, within their respective commands.

VII..On all marches, quartermasters, under the orders of their commanding officers will accompany and conduct their trains in a way not to obstruct the movement of troops

VIII..All quartermasters and commissaries will personally attend to the reception and issue of supplies for their commands, and will keep themselves informed of the condition of the depots, roads, and other communications.

IX..All quartermasters and commissaries will report, by letter, on the first of every month, to the chiefs of their respective departments, at Washington, D. C , their station, and generally the duty on which they have been engaged during the preceding month.

By COMMAND OF MAJOR GENERAL HALLECK:

L. THOMAS,
Adjutant General.

GENERAL ORDERS,   WAR DEPARTMENT,
           ADJUTANT GENERAL'S OFFICE,
No. 162.   *Washington, October* 21, 1862.

I..Enlistments into the Regular Army, under General Orders, No. 154, may be made either in the field or in the several States. But not more than ten volunteers will be enlisted from any one Company.

II..The twenty five dollars advance, of the one hundred dollars bounty authorized by section 5th of Act of Congress approved July 22, 1861, and section 5th of Act approved July 29, 1861, and the two dollars premium authorized by the Act approved June 21, 1862, will only be paid to volunteers enlisting into the Regular Army under this order, who have not already received it. Where Recruiting Officers are not furnished with funds. these amounts, or either of them, will be credited to the Soldier on the first muster roll after his enlistment and paid by the Paymaster who pays him.

By ORDER OF THE SECRETARY OF WAR:

L. THOMAS,
Adjutant General.

GENERAL ORDERS,   WAR DEPARTMENT,
                             ADJUTANT GENERAL's OFFICE,
No. 163.   *Washington, October 22, 1862.*

Whenever prisoners of war are released on parole and sent through the lines, the officers who release them will immediately send rolls to the Adjutant General of the Army containing an exact list of the prisoners' names, rank, regiment date, and place of capture, and date of release on parole. These rolls are indispensable in effecting exchanges of prisoners.

BY ORDER OF THE SECRETARY OF WAR:

L. THOMAS,
Adjutant General.

GENERAL ORDERS,   WAR DEPARTMENT,
                             ADJUTANT GENERAL's OFFICE,
No. 165.   *Washington, October 22, 1862.*

I..The allowances granted to witnesses examined before General Courts Martial and Courts of Inquiry, will also be made to those summoned before Military Commissions.

II..Attention is specially directed to the requirement in paragraph 891, General Regulations, that the Record of Courts Martial shall show that the Judge Advocate was duly sworn in the presence of the prisoner; the omission of which invalidates the proceedings.

BY ORDER OF THE SECRETARY OF WAR:

L. THOMAS,
Adjutant General.

GENERAL ORDERS,   WAR DEPARTMENT,
                             ADJUTANT GENERAL's OFFICE,
No. 166.   *Washington, October 23, 1862.*

It appearing that large quantities of government property have been unlawfully disposed of by non-commissioned officers and soldiers, in violation of law and of the Army rules and regulations, it is therefore ordered: That all United States officers commanding posts shall seize all military clothing, blankets, shoes, arms, equipments, and other such supplies, which have been issued by the government to soldiers, and lost or disposed of by them. And it shall be incumbent on any person, not a soldier, who may have any such property in his possession, to prove that he has lawfully acquired possession thereof.

Such property, when seized, will be turned over to a United States Quartermaster, and his receipt in duplicate taken therefor, one of such receipts to be transmitted to the Quartermaster General. The seizure will also be reported to the Adjutant General.

All Provost Marshals appointed by the Department will assist in recovering to the United States this description of public property.

Commanding officers of companies are reminded that it is their duty not only to cause soldiers who are guilty of violating the law forbidding the sale, destruction, or negligent loss of clothing, arms, and public property, to be charged on the Muster Rolls with all the articles improperly lost or disposed of, but also to enforce such other punishment as the nature of their offence may demand.

By ORDER OF THE SECRETARY OF WAR:

L. THOMAS,
Adjutant General.

___

GENERAL ORDERS, WAR DEPARTMENT,
                 ADJUTANT GENERAL'S OFFICE,
No. 167.   *Washington, October* 24, 1862.

Every Commanding Officer of a Detachment, Company, Regiment, or Post, who has any arms in his possession, or under his control, for which he is accountable, shall, within *ten days* after the reception of this order at the camp or post at which he may be stationed, or, if on the march, within twenty days after it has been communicated to him from the headquarters to which he reports, make an inventory, stating—

First. The number of arms for which he is accountable, giving the name or names of the arms.

Second. The calibre of the arms.

Third. Whether they are smooth or rifled.

Fourth. How many are serviceable, and how many require repairs.

Fifth. How many of the arms are in use, and at what place or places those not in use are kept, and what is their condition.

Sixth. The date at which this order was communicated to him.

Such inventory will be signed by the officer making it with his full name, title, and post office address, and be transmitted without delay, by mail, to Brigadier General James W. Ripley, Chief of Ordnance, Washington, D. C., with a letter of advice.

Commanding Officers of Armies, Corps, Divisions, Brigades, Regiments, and Posts, are required to see that this order is enforced in their respective commands, and to report to the Adjutant General whether it has been complied with, stating the names of all officers who fail or neglect to comply with it within the time specified.

BY ORDER OF THE SECRETARY OF WAR:

L. THOMAS,
Adjutant General.

GENERAL ORDERS,   WAR DEPARTMENT,
ADJUTANT GENERAL'S OFFICE,
No. 169.   *Washington, October 27, 1862.*

I.. Hereafter, after every battle, skirmish, or other engagement, the Commanding Officer of each Regiment, Battery, or other detached portion of a Regiment, there present, will, in addition to the lists transmitted through immediate Commanders, promptly forward, *direct to this office,* a correct return of the *killed,* wounded, and missing of his command.

II.. As the *monthly returns* of Regiments, by being transmitted through Brigade Headquarters, are detained and lost, they will hereafter be forwarded *direct* to this office.

BY ORDER OF THE SECRETARY OF WAR:

L. THOMAS,
Adjutant General.

GENERAL ORDERS,   }   WAR DEPARTMENT,
                               ADJUTANT GENERAL'S OFFICE,
  No. 176.   }   *Washington, October* 31, 1862.

I..The Commissary General of Prisoners has charge of the U. S. officers and men on parole; and correspondence relating to them, as well as all details concerning them, will pass through him.

     o   o   o   o   o   o   o   o

BY ORDER OF THE SECRETARY OF WAR:

                     L. THOMAS,
                           Adjutant General.

GENERAL ORDERS,   }   WAR DEPARTMENT,
                               ADJUTANT GENERAL'S OFFICE,
  No. 177.   }   *Washington, October* 31, 1862.

The Regiments and Companies of Volunteer Engineers, recognized by the 20th section of the Act of July 17, 1862, will have the following organization:

REGIMENT OF ENGINEERS—TWELVE COMPANIES.

1 *Colonel.*

1 *Lieutenant Colonel.*

3 *Majors.*   .

1 *Adjutant,* (not an extra Lieutenant)

1 *Quartermaster,* (not an extra Lieutenant.)

1 *Chaplain.*

1 *Surgeon.*

2 *Assistant Surgeons.*

1 *Hospital Steward.*

3 *Quartermaster Sergeants.*

3 *Commissary Sergeants.*

COMPANY OF ENGINEERS.

1 *Captain.*

2 *First Lieutenants.*

1 *Second Lieutenant.*

2 *Musicians.*

10 *Sergeants.*
10 *Corporals.*
64 *Artificers.*
64 *Privates.*

BY ORDER OF THE SECRETARY OF WAR:

L. THOMAS,
Adjutant General.

GENERAL ORDERS, }   WAR DEPARTMENT,
               ADJUTANT GENERAL'S OFFICE,
No. 179.   }   *Washington, October 31, 1862.*

Paragraph 1, of "General Orders," No. 92, of October 26, 1861, is so far modified as to require the submission to the Secretary of War of plans for hospital accomodation of the sick only in cases which, in the opinion of the Quartermaster General, or of the Surgeon General, require special action of the Secretary.

BY ORDER OF THE SECRETARY OF WAR:

L. THOMAS,
Adjutant General.

GENERAL ORDER RESPECTING THE OBSERVANCE OF THE SABBATH DAY IN THE ARMY AND NAVY.

EXECUTIVE MANSION,
Washington, November 15, 1862.

The President, Commander-in-Chief of the Army and Navy, desires and enjoins the orderly observance of the Sabbath by the officers and men in the military and naval service. The importance for man and beast of the prescribed weekly rest, the sacred rights of Christian soldiers and sailors, a becoming deference to the best sentiment of a Christian people, and a due regard for the Divine will, demand that Sunday labor in the Army and Navy be reduced to the measure of strict necessity.

The discipline and character of the national forces should not suffer, nor the cause they defend be imperilled, by the profanation of the day or name of the Most High. "At this time of public distress"—adopting the words of Washington in 1776 —" men may find enough to do in the service of God and their country without abandoning themselves to vice and immorality." The first General Order issued by the Father of his Country after the Declaration of Independence, indicates the spirit in which our institutions were founded and should ever be defended : *" The General hopes and trusts that every officer and man will endeavor to live and act as becomes a Christian soldier defending the dearest rights and liberties of his country."*

ABRAHAM LINCOLN.

GENERAL ORDERS,	WAR DEPARTMENT,
	ADJUTANT GENERAL'S OFFICE,
No. 187.	Washington, November 15, 1862.

Major General E. A. Hitchcock, U. S. Volunteers, is detailed as Commissioner for the Exchange of Prisoners of War.

BY ORDER OF THE SECRETARY OF WAR:

E. D. TOWNSEND,
Assistant Adjutant General.

GENERAL ORDERS,	WAR DEPARTMENT,
	ADJUTANT GENERAL'S OFFICE,
No. 189.	Washington, November 18, 1862.

I..Commanding officers of all regiments armed with any muskets, rifles, or carbines, other than the Springfield Rifled Musket, model of 1855-'61, are authorized to detail from their regiments each a competent and skilful mechanic to act as armorer to repair the arms of the regiment.

Suitable tools and the necessary spare parts will be provided by the Ordnance Department.

Accounts for the extra-duty pay allowed by paragraph 902, General Regulations of the Army, for such services, will be made, in duplicate, on Form No. 13, Ordnance Regulations, special blanks for which must be obtained from the Ordnance Bureau, City of Washington. These accounts, duly certified by the Regimental Commander, *and accompanied by a certified copy of the Regimental Order placing the armorer on extra duty,* will be forwarded to the Chief of Ordnance, Washington, D. C., or to the Chief Ordnance officer at the headquarters of the Department, or Army, for their approval; and, when so approved, will be paid at the nearest Arsenal, or by any Disbursing Officer of Ordnance in the field.

Requisitions for one set of armorer's tools, and such spare parts as are required, *stating particularly the kind and calibre of the arm,* will be made by Commanders of Regiments entitled to armorers under this order, which requisitions, after being duly approved at the Department, or Army, headquarters, will be forwarded to the Chief of Ordnance, at Washington, for final action.

II..To meet the provisions of the above order, paragraph 905, General Regulations, is amended by inserting after the word "Companies," in the third line, the following: "and armorers for repairing arms of regiments serving as Infantry, or Cavalry."

III..The fourth line of paragraph 1023, General Regulations, is modified to read as follows: "may require—the *sale* of ordnance and ordnance stores excepted," &c.

By order of the Secretary of War:

E. D. TOWNSEND,
Assistant Adjutant General.

Form No 13.

THE UNITED STATES to *Private* ——————, C. ——, —— *Reg t* ——, *Vols.* Dr.

—————— , 186 .

I CERTIFY that Private —— was actually employed at work as an Armorer for the Regiment named for the number of days charged in the annexed account; that the labor was actually performed, and was necessary to keep in order the public arms in use by the Regiment.

APPROVED :

——————————— ,
Comd'g Reg't.

APPROVED :

——————————— ,

——————————— ,
Chief of Ordnance.

APPROPRIATION.

ORDNANCE, ORDNANCE STORES, &c.

For services as Armorer for the —— Regiment —— Volunteers, from the —— day of ——, 186 , to the —— day of ——, 186 , being —— days, at 40 cents per day ------------------

(See paragraph 902, General Regulations of the Army.)

DOLLARS----

186 .

o

(*Date the account on the last day on which service was rendered.

RECEIVED from ——, —— dollars —— cents, in full of the above account.

——, 186 . ——————————— .

(ORIGINAL.) (*Sign here.*)

GENERAL ORDERS,   WAR DEPARTMENT,
                 ADJUTANT GENERAL's OFFICE,
No. 190.   *Washington, November* 19, 1862.

When there is no mustering officer to certify to the accounts payable by the Commissary General of Subsistence, according to the first paragraph of "General Orders," No. 121, the affidavit of the claimant, supported by the certificate of the Commissioner for drafting, will be required before payment of the account.

BY ORDER OF THE SECRETARY OF WAR:

E. D. TOWNSEND,
Assistant Adjutant General.

GENERAL ORDERS,   WAR DEPARTMENT,
                 ADJUTANT GENERAL's OFFICE,
No. 191.   *Washington, November* 19, 1862.

I..The following announcement is officially made of the result of the recent exchange of prisoners of war arranged at Aiken's Landing, November 11, 1862, and all officers and enlisted men interested will be governed accordingly:

First. All officers and enlisted men in the United States service, who have been captured and paroled in Virginia and Maryland up to November 1, 1862, except the officers and enlisted men captured and paroled in September, 1862, at Harper's Ferry, and not hereinafter mentioned, and all deliveries of prisoners up to November 11, 1862, made to the United States authorities in the Peninsula and its adjacent waters, are included in this exchange.

Second. All officers and enlisted men captured and paroled at Santa Rosa Island October 4, 1861.

Third. All officers and enlisted men captured and paroled at Chambersburg, Pa , October 4, 1862.

Fourth. The Seventy-first Ohio Volunteers, captured at Clarksville, Tenn.

Fifth. Officers and enlisted men captured at South Mills, N. C.

Sixth. One hundred and four non-commissioned officers and privates belonging to the Second United States Cavalry, First United States

Infantry, Sixth United States Cavalry, Second United States Artillery, Third United States Infantry, Sixth, Eighth, Tenth, Eleventh, Twelfth, Seventeenth United States Infantry, Fourth and Fifth United States Artillery, sent from Annapolis, Md., to Fort Columbus, N. Y., October 4, 1862.

Seventh. All officers and enlisted men captured at or near Richmond and Lexington, Ky., by the forces under the command of General E. Kirby Smith.

Eighth. All officers and enlisted men delivered to Captains Lazelle and Swan, on the 1st, 5th, 7th, 12th, and 26th of September, 1862, and the 18th of October, 1862.

Ninth. All officers and enlisted men paroled at Cumberland Gap on the 2d and 11th of October, 1862.

Tenth. All officers and men of Indiana troops captured at Mumfordsville, Ky., September 17, 1862.

Eleventh. Company A and Company F, 5th New York Artillery; detachment of 8th New York Cavalry; 39th, 111th, 115th, 125th, and 126th Regiments New York Volunteers; all captured at Harper's Ferry, and now at Camp Douglas.

Twelfth. All officers and men of Rigby's and Von Sepien's Indiana batteries taken at Harper's Ferry.

All paroled officers and soldiers who come under any of the foregoing classes, now absent from the several camps of rendezvous established in par. 3, of "General Orders," No. 72, of 28th June, from the War Department, whether with or without leave, except in cases of sick leave granted by the proper authority, will immediately repair to camps as follows, viz: Those in New England to Camp Joe Hooker, Lakeville, Mass ; those in New York and Pennsylvania to the Camp at Elmyra, N. Y.; those in Ohio to Camp Wallace, near Columbus ; those in Illinois to Camp Butler, Ill.; those in Michigan to Camp Backus, Mich.; those in Wisconsin and Minnesota to Camp Randall, near Madison ; and all others in Western States to Camp Benton, Mo.

The Commanders of the several Camps named, except Camp Wallace, O , Camp Parole, at Annapolis, and Benton Barracks, Mo., will, from time to time, as sufficient numbers are assembled, forward them to the General Camps established in "General Orders," No. 70, Camp Wallace being substituted for Camp Chase.

The paroled troops in Indiana, absent from Camp Morton, or other camps established by Governor Morton, not on sick leave, will immediately repair to the camps at which their regiments are stationed, or to Camp Morton if the regiment is in the field. The regiments at these camps will receive special instructions.

Military Commandants and Recruiting Officers in the different States will furnish transportation to all paroled officers and soldiers who are to report under this order, and will furnish the names of all persons so provided, with the amount paid for each, to the Commander of the Camp to which they are sent, who will forward it, adding any additional amount furnished for transportation, to the Commander of the General Camp, to be finally entered upon the company rolls, unless it is shown that the absence was authorized. The transportation thus paid by Recruiting Officers will be refunded by the Quartermaster's Department.

Commanders of Camps temporarily established for the accommodation of paroled troops, who are now exchanged, will immediately forward all who may be present to the nearest of the General Camps above named.

    o   o   o   o   o   o   o

Individual certificates of exchange are not given. The foregoing order covers all cases.

By order of the Secretary of War :

E. D. TOWNSEND,
Assistant Adjutant General.

GENERAL ORDERS, }   WAR DEPARTMENT,
                  ADJUTANT GENERAL's OFFICE,
No. 192. }   *Washington, November* 20, 1862.

Commandants of Corps, Divisions, and Brigades, are hereby required to have a special inspection of the Cavalry of their respective commands, within ten days from the date of this order, and report to this

146

Department the names of all officers whose cavalry horses appear to have been neglected, or be unfit for duty, to the end that such officers may be promptly dismissed from the service.

By order of the Secretary of War:

E. D. TOWNSEND,
Assistant Adjutant General.

GENERAL ORDERS,   WAR DEPARTMENT,
                 Adjutant General's Office,
No. 193.   *Washington, November* 22, 1862.

I..All persons now in military custody who have been arrested for discouraging volunteer enlistments, opposing the draft, or for otherwise giving aid and comfort to the enemy in States where the draft has been made or the quota of volunteers and militia has been furnished, shall be discharged from further military restraint.

II..Persons who, by authority of the military commander or Governor in rebel States, have been arrested and sent from such State for disloyalty or hostility to the government of the United States, and are now in military custody, may also be discharged upon giving their parol to do no act of hostility against the government of the United States, nor render aid to its enemies. But all such persons shall remain subject to military surveillance and liable to arrest on breach of their parol. And if any such persons shall prefer to leave the loyal States on condition of their not returning again during the war, or until special leave for that purpose be obtained from the President, then such person shall, at his option, be released and depart from the United States, or be conveyed beyond the military lines of the United States forces.

III..This order shall not operate to discharge any person who has been in arms against the government, or by force and arms has resisted or attempted to resist the draft, nor relieve any person from liability to trial and punishment by civil tribunals, or by court-martial or military commission, who may be amenable to such tribunals for offences committed.

BY ORDER OF THE SECRETARY OF WAR:

E. D. TOWNSEND,
Assistant Adjutant General.

GENERAL ORDERS,	WAR DEPARTMENT,
No. 194.	ADJUTANT GENERAL'S OFFICE, *Washington, November 24, 1862.*

The Paymaster General is authorized to change the stations of Paymasters within the limits of the pay districts which have been or may be arranged by him, whenever he may deem it necessary for the interests of the service.

BY ORDER OF THE SECRETARY OF WAR:

E. D. TOWNSEND,
Assistant Adjutant General.

GENERAL ORDERS,	WAR DEPARTMENT,
No. 198.	ADJUTANT GENERAL'S OFFICE, *Washington, December 3, 1862.*

I..Mustering and Disbursing Officers are prohibited from paying any accounts for expenses incurred in collecting, drilling, and organizing volunteers, prior to July 1, 1862, unless such accounts shall have been audited and ordered to be paid by the War Department.

II..The intent of paragraph II of General Order, No. 162, current series, has, in some instances, been misunderstood. It is not intended to forbid the payment of bounty. premium, and advance pay to recruits for the old volunteer regiments, viz: those organized prior to July 1, 1862; or to forbid the payment of bounty, premium, or advance pay to a recruit, volunteer, or citizen, who may enlist in the Regular Army, unless said recruit has received said payment before; the object being to avoid paying the same individual twice.

BY ORDER OF THE SECRETARY OF WAR:

E. D. TOWNSEND,
Assistant Adjutant General.

148

GENERAL ORDERS,   }   WAR DEPARTMENT,
ADJUTANT GENERAL'S OFFICE,
No. 200.   }   *Washington, December* 6, 1862.

It is known that many officers are absent from their commands without authority, upon one pretext or another. It is the intention of the Department to dismiss without honor, and without pay, all such officers. They are hereby commanded to return without delay to duty upon pain of having their disgraceful discharge published in newspapers, as well as in General Orders.

BY COMMAND OF MAJOR GENERAL HALLECK:

E. D. TOWNSEND,
Assistant Adjutant General.

———

GENERAL ORDERS,   }   WAR DEPARTMENT,
ADJUTANT GENERAL'S OFFICE,
No. 201.   }   *Washington, December* 8, 1862.

In making out accounts for expenditures connected with the drafting and organization of the militia in the several States, under the act of Congress approved July 17, 1862, the following rules will be observed:

1. The accounts and vouchers must be in duplicate and receipted, and must be transmitted to the Adjutant General of the army, through the Governors of States, with such remarks as they may see fit to make upon them.

2. Each claimant will state distinctly in his account (see form) the items of charge for services or for supplies and all necessary expenditures made by him, for which vouchers must accompany the account.

3. ENROLLING OFFICERS, appointed by the Governors of States. Their accounts must state the number of days they were actually employed, and between what dates; the District; the number of names enrolled by them; and the gross amount of compensation.

These accounts must be certified by the Governor as reasonable and just, and forwarded by him. Under ordinary circumstances the compensation may be three dollars per diem.

4. COMMISSIONERS TO SUPERINTEND DRAFTING; "compensation four dollars per diem for each day actually employed." Their accounts must state the number of days actually employed, and between what dates; the number of names on the rolls transmitted to them; the number of men drafted; the number of men delivered at the camp of rendezvous; the location of the camp, and its distance from the county seat where the draft was made. These accounts to be approved and forwarded by the Governor.

5. EXAMINING SURGEONS; one for each commissioner. Compensation at the rate of four dollars per day *if not commissioned in the United States service.* Their accounts must show the number of days they were actually employed, and between what dates; the number of persons examined; and must be certified by the commissioner for drafting as to the number of those who, on the report of the surgeon, have been exempted, and be approved and forwarded by the Governor. The surgeon must also add his affidavit that he has received no fees, or other consideration, from or on behalf of any person examined by him.

6. SURGEONS who examine drafted men for disability. Their accounts will state the time and date of actual service; the number of men examined; the number and names of men discharged; the reasons therefor; the compensation per diem; and will be approved and forwarded by the Governor, and be sworn to by the Surgeons, as in the case of "Examining Surgeons."

7 COMMANDANTS OF CAMPS. If already in the service of the United States, they will receive the pay of their grade in the service. If not in the United States service, their compensation will be at the rate of five dollars per day. Their accounts must state the number of days, and between what dates, they were actually employed, the location of their camp, and its distance from their residence, and must be approved and forwarded by the Governor.

8. SUBSISTENCE of drafted men before going into camps of rendezvous. These accounts will be made by the parties furnishing subsistence, and will state the number of men subsisted each day, the date, the number supplied with cooked rations on leaving the county seat, and the number of days' supply; also, the price of each ration. These

accounts will be certified by the commissioner, and be approved and forwarded by the Governor.

9. TRANSPORTATION accounts will state the date, number of men transported to camps of rendezvous, and distance travelled, and will be certified by the commissioner in charge of the men, and be approved and forwarded by the Governor.

10. PERSONS DISCHARGED, for disability or illegal draft, will be transported from camps of rendezvous to the county seat whence they came, on passes given by the commandant of the camp, stating name, date, cause of discharge, and distance travelled. These passes will form vouchers for transportation accounts, which must be certified as just and proper by the persons making the accounts, and be approved and forwarded by the Governor.

BY ORDER OF THE SECRETARY OF WAR:

E. D. TOWNSEND,

Assistant Adjutant General.

Form of Voucher and Sub-voucher.

THE UNITED STATES

To ——— ——— ——— ———, DR.

Date.		Amount.	
186 .		Dolls.	Cts.
	[Here enumerate separately the items for which payment is to be made, or number of days employed and rate per diem; carry out the charge for each item; sum up all and enter the gross amount in the form of receipt at the foot of the account.]		
	Total........ ......$		

[Here insert the certificate required in each case by the directions laid down in the foregoing order. The approvals of Governors and affidavits (when required) will be made on the back of this voucher.]

Received —— this —— day of —— of ——, —— dollars and
—— cents, in full of the above account.

——— ———.

——— ———.

$ ———.

[DUPLICATED.]

———

GENERAL ORDERS, ⎫   WAR DEPARTMENT,
           ⎬   ADJUTANT GENERAL'S OFFICE,
No. 202. ⎭   *Washington, December* 9, 1862.

The accompanying statements of the cost of clothing and camp and
garrison equipage for the Army of the United States, to govern until
further orders, with the allowance of clothing to each soldier during
his enlistment and his proportion for each year, also of the cost of
horse equipments, are published for the information and guidance of
all concerned.

BY ORDER OF THE SECRETARY OF WAR:

E. D. TOWNSEND,
Assistant Adjutant General.

STATEMENT of the cost of Clothing, Camp, and Garrison Equipage for the Army of the United States until further orders, with the allowance of clothing to each soldier during enlistment, and his proportion for each year.

Money columns are expressed in $ (dollars) and c. (cents).

CLOTHING	Engineer Troops	Hospital Stewards	Ordnance Sergeants	Ordnance Mechanics	Cavalry	Light Artillery	Artillery	Infantry	First	Second	Third	Fourth	Fifth	Allowance for 5 years
Uniform Hat	1 68	1 68	1 68	1 68	1 68	1 68	1 68	1 68	1	1	1	1	1	5
" Feather	15	15	15	15	15	15	15	15	1	1	1	1	1	5
" Cord and tassel	14	14	14	14	14	14	14	14	1	1	1	1	1	5
" Eagle	2	2	2	2	2	2	2	2						
" Castle	10													
" Shell and flame			5	5										
" Crossed sabres					3									
" Crossed cannon						3	3							
" Bugle								3						
" Letter							1	1						
" Number					1		1	1						
Cap, (Light Artillery)						1 06								
" Tulip						8								
" Cord and tassel						75								
" Plate						4								
" Rings, pairs of						8								
" Hair plume						75								
Forage Cap	56	56	56	56	56	56	56	56	1	1	1	1	1	5
" Cover	18	18	18	18	18	18	18	18						
Uniform Coat, Musicians'	7 45						7 45	7 45	2	1	2	1	2	8
" Privates'	7 21	7 21	7 21	7 21			7 21	7 21	2	1	2	1	2	8
" Jacket, Musicians'					5 97	5 97			2	1	2	1	2	8
" Privates'					5 55	5 55			2	1	2	1	2	8

Item											
Chevrons, pairs, N. C. S.											
" " 1st Sergeants'									13	3	2	3	2	3
" " Sergeants'									13					
" " Corporals'									13					
Caducens												
Shoulder Scales, pairs, N. C. S.									15	3	3	3	3	3
" " " Sergeants'									11	2	2	2	2	3
" " " Privates'									20	4	4	4	4	4
Trowsers, Sergeants'	35	3 75							20	4				4
" Corporals'	24													
" Privates'	20													
Sash												
Flannel Sack Coat, (unlined)	50	50	50							1		1		1
" " " (lined)	50	50	50											
Knit Jackets	3 75	3 75	3 75						2					2
Flannel Shirts	3 75									1	1	1		1
Knit	3 55													
Flannel Drawers	1 84													
Knit	2 40													
Stockings	3 14													
Bootees, sewed	2 70													
" pegged	1 46													
Boots, sewed	1 30													
" pegged	95													
Great Coats	1 00													
" Straps, pairs	32													
Blankets, woollen	2 05													
" painted	1 48													
" rubber												
Poncho, painted												
" rubber												
Leather Stocks	10													1
Leggins, leather												
" linen	1 58													
Overalls												
Stable Frocks										5	1		1		5
Talmas										2			1		2

Camp and garrison equipage.

Knapsacks and straps..............	$2 14	Drum cord.......................		$0 30
Haversacks, unpainted............	48	" snares, sets............		16
" enamelled and painted	56	" case...................		38
Canteen, complete	44	Wall tent	$35 00	
" strap, leather............	15	" " fly	17 00	
Bedsacks, single	3 00	" " poles, sets........	87	
" double	3 15	" " pins, sets.........	39	
Mosquito bars	3 15			53 26
Axe.............................	83	Sibley tent	60 00	
" helve..........	12	" " pole and tripod...	3 40	
" sling........................	63	" " pins, sets	31	
Hatchet	32			63 71
" helve	3	" " stove		2 62
" sling	35	Hospital tent	87 54	
Spade.	70	" " fly	33 20	
Shovel...........................	65	" " poles, sets	2 00	
Pickaxe	67	" " pins, sets	1 00	
" helve	11			123 74
Camp kettle.....................	55	Common tent	21 50	
Mess pan...	23	" " poles, sets	70	
Iron pot	1 15	" " pins, sets	25	
Garrison flag	43 00			22 45
" " halliard..............	3 25	Shelter tent, complete		3 25
Storm flag	17 00	Tent pins, hospital, large..........		3
Recruiting flag...................	6 50	" wall "		2
" " halliard	1 00	" common, small.........		1
Guidon........................	12 00	Regimental book, order	1 33	
Camp color	2 28	" " letter	1 35	
Standard, for mounted regiments..	30 00	" " index.....	1 46	
National color, artillery & infantry.	42 00	" " descriptive	2 10	
Regimental " "	63 00			6 26
Color belt and sling..............	4 50	Post book, morning report...	50	
Trumpet, with extra mouth-piece .	3 37	" guard report	86	
Bugle, " " "	3 00	" order	50	
Cords and tassels for trumpets or		" letter	50	
bugles.........................	90			2 36
Fife, "B" or "C"..................	50	Company book, clothing	2 00	
Drum, complete..................	5 50	" " descriptive .	1 38	
" head, batter	75	" " order......	52	
" " snare	28	" " morn. report	1 50	
" sling	40			3 40
" sticks, pairs	22	Regimental book, general order....		1 30
" " carriage	52	Record book, for target practice...		56

Camp and garrison equipage.

Knapsacks and straps	$2 14
Haversacks, unpainted	48
" enamelled and painted	56
Canteen, complete	44
" strap, leather	15
Bedsacks, single	3 00
" double	3 15
Mosquito bars	3 15
Axe	83
" helve	12
" sling	63
Hatchet	32
" helve	3
" sling	35
Spade	70
Shovel	65
Pickaxe	67
" helve	11
Camp kettle	55
Mess pan	23
Iron pot	1 15
Garrison flag	43 00
" " halliard	3 25
Storm flag	17 00
Recruiting flag	6 50
" " halliard	1 00
Guidon	12 00
Camp color	2 28
Standard, for mounted regiments..	30 00
National color, artillery & infantry.	42 00
Regimental " "	63 00
Color belt and sling	4 50
Trumpet, with extra mouth-piece .	3 37
Bugle, " " "	3 00
Cords and tassels for trumpets or bugles	90
Fife, "B" or "C"	50
Drum, complete	5 50
" head, batter	75
" " snare	28
" sling	40
" sticks, pairs	22
" " carriage	52

Drum cord		$0 30
" snares, sets		16
" case		38
Wall tent	$35 00	
" " fly	17 00	
" " poles, sets	87	
" " pins, sets	39	
		53 26
Sibley tent	60 00	
" " pole and tripod	3 40	
" " pins, sets	31	
		63 71
" " stove		2 62
Hospital tent	87 54	
" " fly	33 20	
" " poles, sets	2 00	
" " pins, sets	1 00	
		123 74
Common tent	21 50	
" " poles, sets	70	
" " pins, sets	25	
		22 45
Shelter tent, complete		3 25
Tent pins, hospital, large		3
" wall		2
" common, small		1
Regimental book, order	1 35	
" " letter	1 35	
" " index	1 46	
" " descriptive	2 10	
		6 26
Post book, morning report	50	
" guard report	86	
" order	50	
" letter	50	
		2 36
Company book, clothing	2 00	
" " descriptive .	1 38	
" " order	52	
" " morn. report	1 50	
		5 40
Regimental book, general order....		1 30
Record book, for target practice...		56

TABLE *specifying the Money Value of Clothing allowed to the Army of the United States.*

	NON-COM. STAFF. CHIEF MUSICIAN.		FIRST SERGEANT.			SERGEANT.				HOSPITAL STEWARD.	CORPORAL.			MUSICIAN.			ARTIFICER AND PRIVATE.			
	Cavalry and Light Arty.	Artillery and Infantry.	Cavalry or Lt. Artillery.	Artillery Infantry.	Engineers.	Cavalry or Lt. Artillery.	Artillery Infantry.	Engineers.	Ordnance.	Cavalry or Lt. Artillery.	Artillery Infantry.	Engineers.	Cavalry or Lt. Artillery.	Artillery Infantry.	Engineers.	Cavalry or Lt. Artillery.	Artillery Infantry.	Engineers.	Ordnance.	Cavalry or Lt. Artillery.	Artillery Infantry.
First year......	$64 91	$60 71	$45 05	$61 93	$60 55	$62 45	$39 97	$69 33	$60 77	$62 93	$52 75	$60 07	$60 15	$60 15	$52 66	$58 15	$61 99	$58 13	$59 95	$59 95	$61 13	$57 67
Second year....	34 69	34 37	35 11	34 31	34 83	33 81	33 37	34 84	34 27	33 70	33 26	33 92	34 80	33 66	33 22	32 86	33 48	32 86	34 20	34 20	33 06	32 62
Third year.....	51 82	51 18	52 40	52 66	49 96	49 86	48 38	49 74	50 18	49 64	48 16	49 48	49 66	49 56	48 08	47 56	49 60	47 56	48 68	48 88	48 50	47 08
Fourth year....	34 69	34 27	53 11	34 31	34 93	33 81	33 37	34 84	34 27	33 70	33 96	33 92	34 80	33 66	33 22	32 86	33 48	32 86	34 90	34 90	33 06	32 62
Fifth year......	48 27	48 48	47 11	46 96	46 36	44 51	44 68	46 04	46 48	44 29	44 46	43 78	43 96	34 21	44 38	43 86	44 05	43 86	44 96	44 96	43 21	43 36
	229 48	226 97	234 84	229 89	226 07	224 44	218 77	225 79	225 97	223 56	217 89	223 17	225 37	213 94	217 36	213 29	222 60	215 99	221 97	221 97	219 04	213 37

The allowance to Volunteer troops is at the rate of $42 per annum.

Statement of the cost of horse equipments, pattern 1859.

NAMES OF PARTS.	Price per piece.	Price per set.	Amount.
SADDLE.			
Saddle tree, covered with raw hide, with metal mountings attached	$3 87	$3 87	
Saddle flaps, with brass screws, each	1 18	2 36	
Back straps, with screws, rivets, and D's, each	52	1 04	
Girth strap, long	36	36	
" " short	23	23	
Cloak straps, each	17	1 02	
Stirrup leathers, each	57	1 14	
Sweat leathers, each	30	60	
Stirrups, with hoods, each	38	76	
Carbine socket and strap	47	47	
Saddle bags	3 50	3 50	
Crupper	1 01	1 01	
Girth	66	66	
Surcingle	1 16	1 16	
Total cost			$18 18
BRIDLE.			
*Bit, No. 1, $3 50 } average per 100 sets			
†Bit, Nos. 2, 3, and 4, $2 80 }	2 94	2 94	
Brass scutcheon, with company letter, each	5	10	
Reins	55	55	
Head piece	67	67	
Front	16	16	
Curb chain, with hooks	14	14	
Curb chain safe	4	4	
Total cost			4 60
HALTER.			
Head stall, complete	1 55	1 55	
Hitching strap	48	48	
Total cost			2 03
WATERING BRIDLE.			
Snaffle bit, chains, and toggles	50	50	
Watering rein	56	56	
Total cost			1 06
Spurs	20	40	
Spur straps	10	20	
Total cost			60
Currycomb	20	20	
Horse brush	67	67	
Picket pin	13	13	
Lariat rope	61	61	
Total cost			1 61
Total cost of equipment			28 08
Blanket for cavalry service, dark, with orange border, 3 lbs., at 75 cents per lb	2 25	2 25	
Blanket for artillery, scarlet, with dark blue border, 3 lbs. at 70 cents per lb	2 10	2 10	
Nose bag	1 25	1 25	
Hitching strap	25	25	

* NOTE.—No. 1 is Spanish; Nos. 2, 3, and 4 are American.
† NOTE.—For officers' scutcheons, gilt, 15 cents each.

156

Table showing the prices of malleable iron parts, buckles, D's, rings, &c.

Tabular number o piece.	Place where used and kind of buckle.	Number required in each set.	Size.	Price.
			Inch.	Cts.
1	Girth, with roller, round	1	2	2
2	Stirrup, bar, flattened	2	1.375	2
3	Halter, bar, flattened	1	1.125	2
4	Girth and surcingle, roller, round	2	1.5	2
5	Bridle, crupper, bar	4	.75	1
6	Throat lash, saddle bags, cloak straps, and carbine socket, bar	12	.625	1
7	Halter, square	2	1.6×1.2	2
8	Halter ring.	2	1.7	2
9	Ring for crupper and saddle tree	5	1.25	1
10	Halter bolt	1	1.10	1
11	Foot staples	6	.9	1
12	D's, back straps, and girths.	3	1 85	4
13	Saddle bags' stud	1	1×0.4	2

GENERAL ORDERS, } WAR DEPARTMENT,
ADJUTANT GENERAL'S OFFICE,
No. 212. } *Washington, December 23, 1862.*

I.-Hereafter the chiefs of the respective Bureaux in the War Department will designate the officers to be assigned as Adjutant General, Quartermaster, Commissary of Subsistence, and Inspector General for each Army Corps, in accordance with section 10 of the Act approved July 17, 1862. These officers will, when once assigned, remain permanently attached to their respective Corps without regard to the movements of Corps Commanders, unless otherwise assigned by the President.

II.-The Aides-de-Camp authorized for Corps Commanders by the Act quoted above will be appointed by the President, by and with the advice and consent of the Senate, on the recommendation of the Corps Commanders. They may accompany the Generals for whom they were appointed in his change of duties or station ; but when he is assigned to a command inferior to an Army Corps, their appointments as Aides-de-Camp for a Corps Commander will be revoked, and they will fall back upon the commission previously held.

III..The Assistant Adjutants General of divisions and brigades will hereafter remain permanently attached to the commands to which once assigned; and will not be considered as part of the personal staff of the General on whose recommendation they were appointed.

All Assistant Adjutants General of Volunteers, now off duty, or not on their appropriate duty with some corps, division, or brigade of Volunteers, will immediately report their names and address to this office, that they may be assigned to duty.

IV..Hereafter all applications by General Officers for the appointment either of Assistant Adjutants General or officers of the Quartermaster or Commissary Departments, will be transmitted through the headquarters of the Army to which they are attached, and will not thence be forwarded to this office, unless there are no disposable Staff Officers of the description asked for, who can be assigned by the Commander of the Army to the General Officer making application for them.

No General Officer will, therefore, be permitted to make such application while detached from, or, if newly appointed, until he shall have joined, the Army with which he is to serve.

V..The only members of their Staff whom General Officers are authorized to take with them, in future, when detached from, or otherwise leaving their commands, are their ordinary Aides-de-Camp—those selected in accordance with the Acts of July 22 and 29, 1861, sections 3 and 4, respectively, and of July 17, 1862, section 10.

By order of the Secretary of War:

L. THOMAS,
Adjutant General.

GENERAL ORDERS, }   WAR DEPARTMENT,
ADJUTANT GENERAL'S OFFICE,
No. 216. }   *Washington, December* 26, 1862.

Hereafter, as soon as the muster into service of any force is completed, the mustering officers will report the fact to the Commanding

General of the Department in which they are serving. They will, at the same time, transmit a return of the troops, and state when they will be equipped and ready to march.

BY ORDER OF THE SECRETARY OF WAR:

L. THOMAS,
Adjutant General.

The foregoing orders are reprinted for the information of all concerned.

BY ORDER OF THE SECRETARY OF WAR:

Assistan Adjutant General.

WAR DEPARTMENT,
ADJUTANT GENERAL'S OFFICE,
Washington, March , 1863.

www.ingramcontent.com/pod-product-compliance
Lightning Source LLC
Chambersburg PA
CBHW030327270326
41926CB00010B/1528